Understanding Hezekiah of Judah

Rebel King and Reformer

Mordechai Cogan

cartaJerusalem

First published in 2017 by
CARTA Jerusalem

11 Rivka Street, P.O.B. 2500,
Jerusalem 9102401, Israel
E-mail: carta@carta.co.il
www.carta-jerusalem.com

Quotations from the Hebrew Bible follow the New Revised Standard Version unless otherwise indicated.

Great care has been taken to establish sources of illustrations. If inadvertently we omitted to do so, due credit will be given in the next edition.

ISBN: 978-965-220-882-8

Printed in the United States of America

CONTENTS

1. INTRODUCTION

© Eilat Mazar, Photo: Ouria Tadmor

The inscription on this seal impression (bulla) reads: "Hezekiah, (son of) Ahaz, king of Judah." From the Ophel, Jerusalem (courtesy Eilat Mazar).

Tradition remembers Hezekiah, son of Ahaz, as one of the most righteous kings to have ruled over the Kingdom of Judah. In the estimation of the author of the biblical Book of Kings:

> He (Hezekiah) did what was right in the sight of the Lord just as his ancestor David had done.... He trusted in the Lord, the God of Israel; so that there was no one like him among all the kings of Judah after him, or among those who were before him. (2 Kgs 18:3, 5)

Indeed Hezekiah was the first king of the House of David to carry out a wide-ranging reform of the Israelite cult that resulted in the elevation of the Temple of Jerusalem to the status of the central shrine of the kingdom. More than a half-millennium later, in the Hellenistic period, his piety was recalled by the wisdom teacher Ben Sirah, who included Hezekiah among the praiseworthy ancestors of Israel, alongside David and Josiah (cf. Sirach 48:17–22; 49:4).

The twenty-nine year reign of Hezekiah (727–698 BCE) stands out as one of the momentous periods in the history of Judah, coming as it did at the time when the Assyrian Empire had turned to strengthening its hold on the Mediterranean coast from the border of Egypt to Anatolia. Though at first Hezekiah adopted the policy of submission to Assyria initiated by his father, he later rejected the noninvolvement in foreign intrigues urged upon him by the prophet Isaiah and rebelled against Assyria (2 Kgs 18:7), perhaps more than once. And it was the rebellion against Sennacherib in 701 BCE that almost brought the deathblow on both dynasty and city. However, in the end, Hezekiah and Jerusalem were spared in what was later perceived as an act of divine salvation that became the source of the city's aggrandizement in the decades and generations that followed.

It is the story of this much-praised scion of the House of David and the city of Jerusalem from which he ruled that is traced in the following exposition.

(opposite) Aerial view of the Temple Mount, looking northwest (photo Samuel Magal).

2. SOURCES FOR THE STUDY OF THE REIGN OF HEZEKIAH

Unlike most periods in the history of ancient Israel, the reign of Hezekiah of Judah (727–698 BCE) is rich with extensive biblical and extra-biblical documentation. This plethora of material presents us with a challenge, for the sources are far from being objective reports of the events described. Like texts from any period of history, they were written by interested parties who set down the picture as they perceived it, reflecting their personal ideology and that of their particular circle. As Edward Hallett Carr reminds us: "In the first place, the facts of history never come to us 'pure,' since they do not and cannot exist in a pure form: they are always refracted through the mind of the recorder."[1] Thus the modern readers of ancient texts should not be surprised when they encounter multiple points of view in what is a variegated past, for they ought to be aware that objectivity can never be fully achieved.

The major source for the days of Hezekiah is the biblical Book of Kings (2 Kgs 18–20), written towards the end of the seventh century BCE, shortly before the end of the Judean monarchy. A century had passed since the heady days of Hezekiah's reign, and the viewpoint of the author of Kings derived from the Deuteronomistic circle active at the court of King Josiah. This circle of literati held that YHWH, the God of Israel, was the one god, who was to be worshiped at the single site in Jerusalem, His chosen city. Accordingly, because Hezekiah had undertaken a reform of the Israelite cult in line with the Deuteronomic ideology, he was reckoned a positive, god-fearing monarch. The main goal of his reform was the closing of all shrines and altars in the towns and villages of Judah (2 Kgs 18:3–4), leaving the Temple of Jerusalem as the sole site for serving the Lord. Hezekiah's piety earned him divine support in all his undertakings, especially during his rebellion against Assyria (2 Kgs 18:7–8). Considerable attention is devoted to this event—it is reported in one of the longest accounts in the Book of Kings; obviously the rebellion and the ensuing war were considered to have been important moments in the history of Judah.

The author of Kings made use of a variety of texts in telling the story of this rebellion. Among them: (1) a short chronicle-like report of the successful invasion of Judah by the Assyrian king, Sennacherib, that led Hezekiah to surrender and pay hefty reparations (2 Kgs 18:13–16); (2) a prophetic account in which an Assyrian high official, Rabshakeh, appears before the walls of Jerusalem and calls for the city's surrender. In his despair, Hezekiah turns to Isaiah for help, and the prophet predicts Sennacherib's imminent retreat and assassination, a prophecy that is reported to have been fulfilled (2 Kgs 18:17–19:9a; 36–37); (3) a second prophetic account highlights Hezekiah's praying to the Lord when faced with the option of surrender or defeat. In response, Isaiah condemns haughty Assyria and predicts the saving of Jerusalem and its king. That very night, the enemy army was miraculously annihilated (cf. 2 Kgs 19:9b–35). The message of all three of these texts: Jerusalem, the city of the Lord's dwelling, and the Davidic king were under divine protection and were therefore saved.

Another recital of Hezekiah's reign is given in the biblical Book of Chronicles (2 Chron 29–32), a composition that dates to the close of the Persian period, some 200 years after the Book of Kings. The Chronicles narrative is based on the presentation given in the Book of Kings, but it has been adapted to present a different message to a later audience. The many new elements in this telling of the story are most likely the creation of the Chronicler.

Complementing these historiographic reports are a number of prophecies of Isaiah and Micah, both of whom were active during the reign of Hezekiah (Isa 1:4–9; 22:1–14; 31:1–3; Micah 1:10–16; 5:4–5). However it is not always possible to relate these prophetic pronouncements to the events known from the other sources.

Beyond the biblical evidence, the most important account is the Assyrian annal inscription of King Sennacherib that describes his campaign to the West in 701 BCE, in particular, against Hezekiah and the kingdom of Judah. From the Assyrian point of view, "Hezekiah the Judean" was a "stubborn and mighty" enemy. Hezekiah thought that he could throw off the yoke of the empire, yet in the end—Sennacherib claims—he, like the other kings who had joined him in rebellion, was forced to surrender to Assyria's superior might (see below, p. 33). In addition to this text, the Assyrian victories in Judah were memorialized in a relief engraved on a wall in Sennacherib's "Palace without Rival" in Nineveh that depicts the battle and capture of the city of Lachish (it is now in the British Museum in London; see below, p. 29).

This trove of written and visual documentation is augmented by the findings from archaeological excavations at major cities attacked by Assyria, notably Lachish and Jerusalem. Taken together, these rich materials make it possible to reconstruct a vivid picture of the last quarter of the eighth century BCE.

3. THE CULT REFORMS OF HEZEKIAH

Remains of the "stelae temple" from Hazor, containing a row of maṣṣēbôt, 13th century BCE (on display at the Israel Museum; photo Edmund Gall, via Wikimedia Commons).

King Hezekiah was one of a small number of Judean monarchs who distinguished themselves by attending to the needs of the Temple of Jerusalem and its cult. As noted in the Book of Kings, these monarchs exercised their authority over the royal shrine, and, due to their devotion to the deity and his clergy, "doing what was right in the sight of the Lord," they were considered praiseworthy. For example, King Asa, in the first quarter of the 9th century, is credited with having "removed all the idols that his ancestors had made. He also removed his mother Maacah from being queen mother, because she had made an abominable image for Asherah" (1 Kgs 15:12–13). Towards the end of that same century, King Joash reorganized the collection and distribution of public donations to the Temple. In what looks like an intrusion on priestly turf, Joash issued a new order so as to put the upkeep of the Temple on a sure footing; from the king's point of view, the Temple staff had neglected its duties (2 Kgs 12:4–16). In contrast to these positive reforms, the installation of a new sacrificial altar by King Ahaz, which replaced the venerable altar that dated back to Solomonic times (2 Kgs 16:10–16), was seen by the author of Kings as untoward, a break with tradition, for which he roundly criticized the king. But with reference to Hezekiah and his reforms, which were no less radical than those of his father Ahaz, the Book of Kings is all praise.

Hezekiah's actions are described concisely and without any explication:

> He removed the high places, broke down the pillars, and cut down the sacred pole. He broke in pieces the bronze serpent that Moses had made, for until those days the people of Israel had made offerings to it; it was called Nehushtan.
>
> (2 Kgs 18:4)

In order to understand the significance of these moves, one should keep in mind that all the appurtenances referred to were part of the accepted cult of the God of Israel as practiced at the end of the eighth century BCE; they were not adoptions of foreign ways. From the very first days of settlement in the Land of Canaan, the Israelites are described as having worshiped God at altars erected throughout the country, located at shrines known as 'high places' (Hebrew: *bāmāh* [singular], *bāmôt* [plural]) that were under the supervision of local priests and Levites. Worship of the God of Israel at the high places continued down to the reign of King Solomon; even he offered sacrifice at the "great *bāmāh*" in Gibeon (1 Kgs 3:4). The building of the Temple in Jerusalem by Solomon did not change this practice; worship at the *bāmôt* continued unabated. But for the author of Kings, this worship was sinful because it violated the law of "the single altar" as set out in Deuteronomy (12:4–12). According to the Deuteronomistic history of Judah, Hezekiah was the first king to move against the local shrines and close them down. In effect, this act centralized the offering of sacrifices on the altar in the Temple of Jerusalem, as it became the sole remaining cult site in the kingdom of Judah.

Moreover, Hezekiah outlawed the continued use of pillars and sacred poles that were associated with the worship of the Lord. The classic precedent for pillars in the Israelite cult is the pillar (Hebrew: *maṣṣēbāh*)—"the stone that he had put under his head"—that Jacob set up in Bethel ("God's house"; cf. Gen 28:18–22). Pillars of this sort were likely seen as memorials, marking the sites of divine revelations. A similar instance of setting up pillars is said to have taken place at the conclusion of the giving of the Law at Mount Sinai: "Moses wrote down all the words of the Lord. He rose early in the morning, and built an altar at the foot of the mountain, and set up twelve pillars, corresponding to the twelve tribes of Israel" (Ex 24:4).

As for the sacred pole (Hebrew: *'ašērāh*), this was a wooden object of some sort, most likely a tree that was planted near the altar (cf. Deut 16:21; Judg 6:25–26). Sacred trees were long known in Israel (cf. Gen 21:33), and some of them shared a common name with the Canaanite goddess Asherah, owing to their association with her cult. The relation of Asherah to the Lord is exemplified by the inscriptions discovered at Kuntillet 'Ajrud (in the Sinai Peninsula, 50 km south of Kadesh Barnea, 15 km east of the border between Egypt and Israel) dated to the

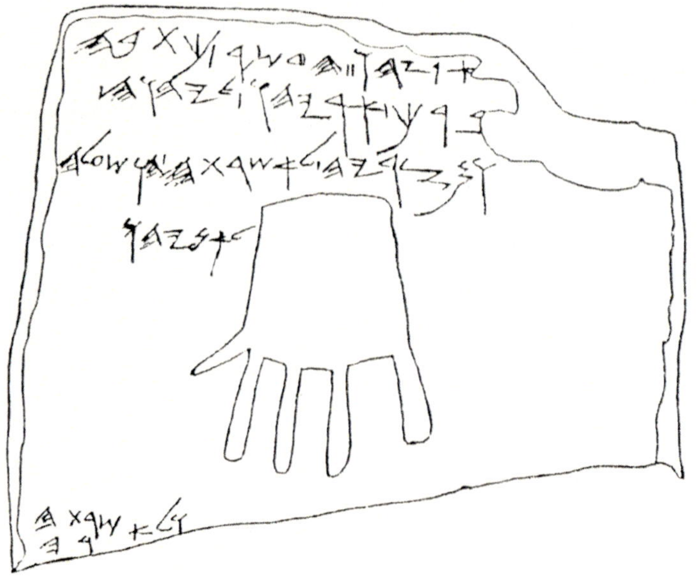

Inscription No. 1 from Makkedah which mentions Asherah (S. Aḥituv, *Echoes from the Past*, pp. 222–223).

early eighth century BCE that read: "I have blessed you to the Lord (YHWH)…and his Asherah."[2] A century later, a similar invocation was inscribed on the wall of a burial cave at Khirbet el-Qôm (biblical Makkedah) in southern Judah.[3] But it is not clear who or what this Asherah was—a sacred cult object or the goddess (who some claim was the Lord's consort)? Whatever the case, Asherah was certainly an accepted feature in the popular religion of ancient Israel.[4]

But perhaps the most surprising of Hezekiah's actions was the extirpation of the Nehushtan. The Nehushtan was a sacred object that claimed a venerable pedigree, reaching back to Israel's forty-year sojourn in the Sinai Peninsula. Tradition told of the repeated complaints of the people because they lacked proper food in the desert. Typical were the words: "Why have you brought us up out of Egypt to die in the wilderness? For there is no food and no water, and we detest this miserable food (i.e., the manna)." The Lord's swift punishment followed, as he "sent poisonous serpents among the people, and they bit the people, so that many Israelites died." Those who survived the attack admitted their sin and were healed by a miraculous remedy: "Moses made a serpent of bronze (Hebrew: *neḥāš neḥošet*), and put it upon a pole; and whenever a serpent (Hebrew: *nāḥāš*) bit someone, that person would look at the serpent of bronze and live" (Num 21:5–8). It appears that the Nehushtan in the Temple of Jerusalem was held to be the bronze serpent of Moses that had accompanied the Israelites from the desert to the Promised Land, where it ultimately became a symbol of worship in its own right. It was this apostasy that made it the object of Hezekiah's violent destruction.

The description of Hezekiah's reforms falls short in a number of aspects. There is no date given for its commencement, nor is there any word of explanation concerning their motivation and goal. This silence on the part of the author of Kings contrasts with the detailed report he gave of the reform undertaken by King Josiah, great-grandson of Hezekiah, in which we read that during repair work on the Temple building, a Book of the Teaching (Hebrew: *sēfer hattôrāh*) was discovered (2 Kgs 22:8). When the book was read out to Josiah, the king ordered the removal of foreign cults, "all the vessels made for Baal, for Asherah, and for all the host of heaven" from the Temple (2 Kgs 23:3–4). Josiah also shut down the high places throughout the kingdom of Judah, "from Geba to Beersheba," and brought all the priests who served at them to Jerusalem, thus expanding the existing staff (2 Kgs 23:8–9). Though not specifically stated, there seems little doubt that the Book of the Teaching that so impressed

A bronze cult standard, plated with silver 14th–13th century BCE, discovered at Hazor, depicting two twisting snakes (NEAEHL).

Group of pottery "pillar figurines," probably representing a fertility goddess (Asherah?), from various sites in Judah, dated to the eighth–seventh centuries BCE (photo Chamberi, via Wikimedia Commons).

Josiah was the Book of Deuteronomy, a suggestion that has been expounded by biblical scholars for over two centuries. Of all the books of the Pentateuch, Deuteronomy stands out as the only one that legislates sacrifice at a single altar in the chosen city. Centralizing sacrifice at one altar was an entirely new idea, radical for its time: in addition to the cleansing of the Land of Canaan of all foreign cults, which was accepted by all groups, Deuteronomic legislation prescribed that all offerings were to be brought to "the place that the LORD your God will choose out of all your tribes as his habitation to put his name there" (Deut 12:5).[5]

It certainly seems that Hezekiah's closing of the high places had been inspired by the altar law of Deuteronomy, but this is nowhere said. Unlike the description of Josiah's reform, there is no mention of a book with regard to Hezekiah, even though most of his actions are spelled out in Deuteronomy—e.g., the elimination of pillars and sacred posts (Deut 16:21–22) and sacrifice at a single altar (Deut 12). Now if the law of centralization had prompted Hezekiah to undertake his reforms—and it does seem like it did—why was such an important fact omitted from the report on Hezekiah in the Book of Kings? The following surmise is worth considering. It may be that the reform ideas expounded in Deuteronomy were only beginning to take shape during Hezekiah's reign. A century later, under Josiah, they had reached completion, were put in writing, and accorded the status of Torah. So while the Teaching of Deuteronomy is not specifically referred to in the case of Hezekiah, one can safely posit Deuteronomic teaching on the subject of a central sanctuary and the imageless worship of the Lord as prompting Hezekiah to act as he did, and for this, the author of the Book of Kings lauded him.

In addition, consideration should be given to the social and political climate of the early years of Hezekiah's reign during which the cultic reforms were likely undertaken. These were the years of the collapse of the northern Kingdom of Israel, its capture by the Assyrians and the exile of a large segment of its population that was followed by the reorganization of the territory as the Assyrian province of *Samerina* (Samaria). For decades prior to the fall of Israel, prophets like Amos and Hosea had warned of the impending crisis because of Israel's moral lassitude and cultic aberrations. Unless a return to the Lord's way was undertaken, these teachers foresaw destruction and exile for all sinners. For example, Hosea intoned:

The inhabitants of Samaria tremble
for the calf of Beth-aven.
Its people shall mourn for it,
and its idolatrous priests shall wail over it,
over its glory that has departed from it.
The thing itself shall be carried to Assyria
as tribute to the great king.
Ephraim shall be put to shame,
and Israel shall be ashamed of his idol.
Samaria's king shall perish,
like a chip on the face of the waters.
The high places of Aven, the sin of Israel,
shall be destroyed. (Hosea 10:5–8)

The idea of an imageless cult reached Judah and became the clarion call for reform in Jerusalem. Micah of Moresheth Gath (in the Judean Shephelah), a contemporary of Isaiah, was active during the reign of Hezekiah. His teachings berated what he considered idolatry in Judah's cult.

In that day, says the LORD,
I will cut off your horses from among you
and will destroy your chariots;

Remains of the holy shrine at Arad, 8th century BCE (photo Mordechai Cogan).

and I will cut off the cities of your land
and throw down all your strongholds;
and I will cut off sorceries from your hand,
and you shall have no more soothsayers;
and I will cut off your images
and your pillars from among you,
and you shall bow down no more
to the work of your hands;
and I will uproot your sacred poles from among you
and destroy your towns. (Micah 5:10–14)

The message was clear: the destruction of the Northern Kingdom was an object lesson. Only by observing the demands of Mosaic Law for a cult devoid of all images, concentrated at a single chosen site, would Judah be spared the fate of Samaria. Hezekiah acted accordingly.

The main benefactors of Hezekiah's reforms were the clergy and coffers of the Temple of Jerusalem. Since its inauguration in the days of Solomon, the Temple had been a royal shrine, serving the needs of the monarch and his household; following the reform, the Temple became a shrine for all Judeans. Pilgrimage to the House of the Lord, God of Israel, in Jerusalem was now seen as a religious duty to be performed three times a year on the occasion of the seasonal festivals (cf. Deut 16:1–17); in addition, all tithes and donations that formerly had supported the high places were now to be rendered at Solomon's Temple (Deut 12:17–18). As a result of these changes, the influence of the Jerusalem priesthood extended beyond the capital to all corners of the kingdom.

Looking back on these reforms from an age that views the centrality of the Temple of Jerusalem as the normal state of affairs, the thought that Hezekiah's reforms were spurned by many in Judah may seem surprising. Yet that was the case. Centuries-old practices had been outlawed by royal fiat, and dissatisfaction was likely to have been great. Among the opposition were the local priests, who without warning and without explanation found themselves unemployed, cut off from position and devoid of income. There was also the populace of the countryside, whose immediate and daily contact with their God had been severed by Hezekiah's edict. Criticism concerning the desirability of the royal altar reform made its way into the prophetic story on the Assyrian attack against Judah (2 Kgs 18:17–19:9). It is imbedded in the speech of the Assyrian official, the Rabshakeh, who is depicted as versed not only in the local language, but also familiar with local customs and politics. He declares that the Lord would withhold help to Judah's war effort because of Hezekiah's closing of the high places that was interpreted as a godless act: "But if you say to me, 'We rely on the LORD our God,' is it not he whose high places and altars Hezekiah has removed, saying to Judah and to Jerusalem, 'You shall worship before this altar in Jerusalem?'" (2 Kgs 18:22). The Rabshakeh's argument gave voice to the opposition in Judah that was displeased with the law of the single altar.[6]

It is difficult to assess the extent of the reform and its success. Some light on this question comes from the archaeological excavations at Tel Beer-sheba, where a large ashlar altar with horned corners was discovered. The stones of the altar were found in secondary use as part of the wall of a storehouse. It is obvious that at some stage, the altar had been downgraded—that is, it had lost its sanctity, allowing for its carefully crafted stones to be utilized in common construction. The archaeological context of the building in which the stones were embedded suggests its erection in the early seventh century BCE, and if so, then the reused altar stones may indicate that Hezekiah's reform had reached as far as the fortress of Beer-sheba on Judah's southern border.[7]

Similar circumstances seem to have prevailed at the royal fortress at Arad in the eastern Negev. The cult installation at Arad consisted of a large sacrificial altar constructed of earth and stones, encased by small field stones, as well as a small shrine with two small incense altars and a pillar. This use of this site was discontinued towards the end of the eighth century by setting the objects on their side and filling in the entire area with earth; after all, these appurtenances had served in cultic function, and so were treated with respect in their careful burial. Though different from the dismantling of the altar at Beer-sheba, it would seem that Hezekiah's reform of the cult also explains the cancellation of sacrifice at Arad.[8]

Hezekiah's dealings with the Temple of Jerusalem went beyond ritual reform. The king is credited with contributions to the enhancement of the building that had been stripped of some of its furnishings by King Ahaz, who had been in straights to meet the vassal payments due the Assyrian king Tiglath-pileser III (2 Kgs 16:17–18). It appears that the royal treasury of Judah had recovered sufficiently for Hezekiah to boast of his great wealth to the members of the Babylonian delegation who had come to Jerusalem: "He showed them all his treasure house, the silver, the gold, the spices, the precious oil, his armory, all that was found in his storehouse" (2 Kgs 20:13); on this visit, see below, page 16. And so, among the gifts Hezekiah made to the Temple was an overlay of gold leaf for its doors and doorposts (2 Kgs 18:16), worthy of a faithful patron of the Lord and His House.

Four-horned altar from Tel Beer-sheba (on display at the Israel Museum; photo Tamarah, via Wikimedia Commons).

4. GOVERNING THE KINGDOM

The territory of the Kingdom of Judah over which Hezekiah ruled encompassed four topographically distinct areas that are spelled out—from south to north and then to the east—in the detailed town list of Judah given in Joshua 15:20–63: (1) the Negeb–Beer-sheba Valley; (2) the Lowland (Hebrew: *Shephelah*)—between the central mountains and the coastal plain; (3) the Hill Country—from Jerusalem southward; (4) the Wilderness–Judean desert. Archaeological study has shown that towards the last quarter of the eighth century BCE, these areas reached new heights of growth and development hitherto unattested. The capital Jerusalem also experienced growth, especially on the southwestern hill opposite the City of David and the Temple Mount; this rural suburb more than doubled the settled area of the city. In the Kidron Valley, a second city wall was built, enclosing the expansion of the city on the east (this is the "double wall" referred to in Isa 22:11; 2 Kgs 25:4).

Because the author of Kings did not consider the subject of the civic affairs pertinent to his didactic presentation of history, he generally passed over this aspect of life in ancient Judah. With one exception, he included information on the organization of the kingdom under Solomon; cf., for example, the lists of Solomon's ministers and district administrators (1 Kgs 4), taxes and state service (1 Kgs 5:6–8; 27–30). But even here, little is known concerning the actual functioning of the governmental apparatus. For the other kings of the Davidic dynasty, there is only the occasional note appended to the survey of their reigns. From the reign of Hezekiah, there is reference in the prophetic stories in 2 Kings 18 to a number of royal ministers, whose offices are known from the Solomonic list: "Eliakim son of Hilkiah, who is in charge of the palace, and Shebnah, the secretary, and Joah son of Asaph, the recorder" (18:18). Shebnah had earlier served as the palace steward, "in charge of the palace," and as Isaiah tells it, he was removed from that high post because of his haughty bearing (Isa 22:15–25). What seem to be the remains of Shebnah's sepulcher and its inscription can still be seen in the Kidron Valley, east of the City of David. The inscription (see image,

Inscription from the sepulcher of "[Sheban]yahu, who is in charge of the palace" (Courtesy of the Trustees of the British Museum).

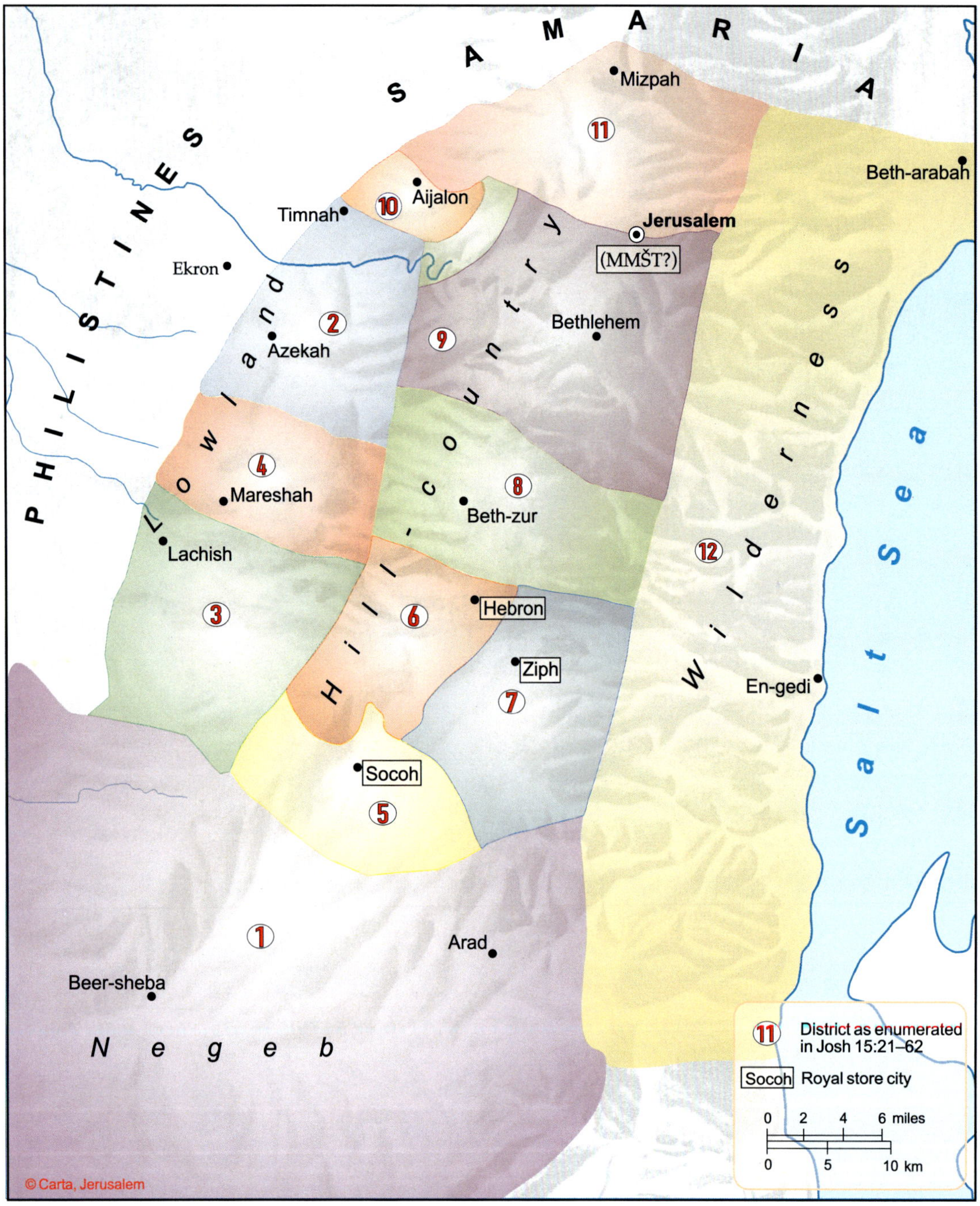

THE KINGDOM OF JUDAH: TOPOGRAPHICAL AND ADMINISTRATIVE DIVISIONS

p. 11) above the entrance to the main chamber reads:

> This is the [burial (chamber) of Sheban]yahu, who is in charge of the palace. There is no silver or gold here; [on]ly [his bones] and the bon[e]s of his handmaid. Cursed be the person who will open this.[9]

The statement concerning Hezekiah's great wealth in the Book of Chronicles makes note of an extensive network of royal centers throughout the realm:

> Hezekiah had very great riches and honor; and he made for himself treasuries for silver, for gold, for precious stones, for spices, for shields, and for all kinds of costly objects; storehouses also for the yield of grain, wine, and oil; and stalls for all kinds of cattle, and sheepfolds. He likewise provided cities for himself, and flocks and herds in abundance.
>
> (2 Chron 32:27–29)

This late description credits Hezekiah with undertaking an extensive program of economic development that would have included the collection of taxes in kind and the distribution of the produce throughout the kingdom. Epigraphic finds from the territory of Judah datable to the end of the eighth century BCE complement this notice and broaden the picture.

At more than a dozen sites throughout Judah—from the Negeb to the Shephelah and into the hill country, as well as in the capital Jerusalem and its northern reaches—over 2,200 engraved jar handles have been recovered. The handles belonged to large ceramic storage jars with a capacity between 45 and 53 liters that likely served as containers for wine, oil or wheat, the main agricultural products of the land. Stamped on the handles are seal impressions with two Hebrew words: the first word is למלך, "(belonging) to the king"; the second one is the name of one of four Judean cities: Hebron (חברון), Ziph (זיף), Socoh (שוכה), MMŠT (ממשת). Hebron is the well-known city at the southern end of the Judean mountains;

(Clockwise, from top left) Royal seals of Socoh, Hebron, and Ziph (S. Aḥituv, *HaKetav veHaMiktav*, Jerusalem 2005).

Ziph is the near-by city to the east of Hebron on the edge of Judean desert (Tel Zif); Socoh is located in the Shephelah (Khirbet ʻAbbad, in the Valley of Elah); the enigmatic MMŠT is unknown, but may mean "government," perhaps indicating a still unidentified royal center. Separating these two words is one of two images: a four-winged scarab beetle (a motif known in Egypt) or a two-winged sun disk. Both images were royal symbols, marking the jars and their contents as state property. There are a small number of exceptions to the preceding description: there are some seals with only the word למלך, some with only a town name, and some with no inscription at all, only one of the images. [Compare the two-winged scarab beetle on Hezekiah's seal; see p. 5.][10]

Petrographic analysis of the handles indicates that material of all the jars came from the same source in the northern Shephelah, which suggests that they were all produced in a central pottery under royal auspices. The date of their manufacture can be determined by their find spots, especially those from Lachish where over 400 למלך seals were discovered; since both images were present on jars recovered in the same level, both images date to the same chronological horizon. Now Lachish Level III was destroyed by Sennacherib in 701 BCE, thereby providing a date in the late 8th century for the seals. A scattering of seals with the two-winged symbol have been recovered in seventh-century levels, an indication of the continued use of this seal type, as well as of older jars that had survived breakage over the years.

A number of proposals have been put forward to explain the use of these storage jars. The למלך seal on their handles clearly indicates the involvement of royal authorities in the manufacture and use of the jars and their contents. It may be that the produce stored in the jars had come from royal estates, that is, the seals identified the vineyards and olive groves as "belonging to the king." Or, as seems more likely, the produce had been delivered by local farmers as taxes at one of the four collection centers named on the seals. From there, the food was shipped to other cities and towns in Judah for use by army and civilian personnel. There is no indication or reason to think that this collection and distribution system was introduced after Hezekiah's rebellion against Assyria in 705 BCE—a common suggestion—as part of the kingdom-wide preparations for the anticipated Assyrian reprisal. For sure, the system would have supported the war effort, but it could well have been introduced years earlier, as the storage jars were typical of the entire eighth century. The application of seals to the handles began late in the century, which suggests that Hezekiah used them as royal propaganda, a means to popularize the achievements of his reign.

A final remark concerning Hezekiah's wealth that included many luxury items, "silver, gold, precious stones, spices" (2 Chron 32:27)—this enumeration suggests that Judah had a commercial interest in the south Arabian trade that passed through the southern port city of Elath on the Red Sea coast and crossed the Negeb, exiting at the seaports of Philistia. (Note that these same luxury products appear as part of the tribute delivered by the queens of the Arabs to Assyria's kings beginning in the late eighth century BCE; see *The Raging Torrent*, nos. 4.06 and 4.08). To accumulate such stores of goods and riches, Hezekiah would have exacted road taxes from the caravans that moved north on their way to the coastal entrepôts.

Royal seal of MMŠT (Courtesy of the Trustees of the British Museum).

5. LITERARY PROPHECY REACHES JUDAH

Among the Jerusalemites who frequented the court of Hezekiah was the prophet Isaiah son of Amoz. Isaiah was no stranger to the royal family. A notable occasion was the visit of the prophet with Ahaz, Hezekiah's father, when he sought to strengthen the king's resolve in the face of a seething political crisis. It seems that Rezin of Damascus and Pekah of Samaria had brought pressure on him to join the anti-Assyrian alliance they were promoting. Isaiah encouraged Ahaz to take a neutral stance—neither to join the rebels nor submit to Tiglath-pileser III (cf. Isa 7:1–9; 2 Kgs 16:5). Trust in the Lord, God of Israel, would see him through the crisis. Decades later, when Hezekiah was under stress due to Sennacherib's demand for surrender, Isaiah brought a similar message: trust in the Lord would bring salvation to city and king (2 Kgs 19:1–7, 32–34). In addition to being a political adviser, Isaiah was a personal counselor to the king. Thus when Hezekiah lay mortally ill, it was Isaiah who brought the promise of the Lord's healing and the extension of the king's life for another fifteen years (2 Kgs 20:1–11).

Isaiah's ministry reached beyond the royal palace. In his public addresses, the prophet introduced a new message to the populace of Judah and Jerusalem. The prophets of previous generations had called for maintaining loyalty to the Lord, God of Israel, worshiping Him alone, and scrupulously shunning the lure of foreign gods and their practices. They warned that abandonment of the Lord would bring dire consequences upon the nation. In this, the teaching of the prophets echoed that of the Torah literature and the great biblical histories. Elijah's career is representative of prophecy of this spirit. But Isaiah spoke of different things.

Like his contemporary Micah of Moresheth-gath in the Judean Shephelah, Isaiah introduced Judeans to the teachings of Amos and Hosea, prophets who had been active in the kingdom of Israel during the two decades prior to the fall of Samaria. The hallmark of these northern literary prophets—a designation more apropos than the customary "classical" prophets—was their call for justice and righteousness in reforming Israelite society. Isaiah took up the cause of Judah's neglected populace, those who worked the land and were robbed and enslaved by the wealthy few whom he censured:

Ah, you who join house to house,
who add field to field,
until there is room for no one but you,
and you are left to live alone
in the midst of the land!
The LORD of hosts has sworn in my hearing:
Surely many houses shall be desolate,
large and beautiful houses, without inhabitant.
For ten acres of vineyard shall yield but one bath,
and a homer of seed shall yield a mere ephah.
(Isa 5:8–10)

A new idolatry had struck root in Judah, the worship of material gain.

According to the new prophetic standard for national well-being, social morality was elevated to the level earlier occupied by cultic duties; but now sacrifice to the Lord, the accepted sign of loyalty to Him, would no longer be the guarantor of the common weal. Moreover, the responsibility of the individual to pursue justice as taught in the Torah of Moses was extended beyond the individual Israelite to embrace the entire nation:

Hear the word of the LORD,
you rulers of Sodom!
Listen to the teaching of our God,
you people of Gomorrah!
What to me is the multitude of your sacrifices?
says the LORD;
I have had enough of burnt offerings of rams,
and the fat of fed beasts;
I do not delight in the blood of bulls, or of lambs, or of goats.
When you come to appear before me,
who asked this from your hand?
Trample my courts no more;
bringing offerings is futile;
incense is an abomination to me.
New moon and Sabbath and calling of convocation—
I cannot endure solemn assemblies with iniquity.
Your new moons and your appointed festivals
my soul hates;
they have become a burden to me,
I am weary of bearing them.
When you stretch out your hands,
I will hide my eyes from you;
even though you make many prayers,
I will not listen;
your hands are full of blood.
Wash yourselves; make yourselves clean;
remove the evil of your doings from before my eyes;
cease to do evil, learn to do good;
seek justice, rescue the oppressed, defend the orphan,
plead for the widow. (Isa 1:10–17)

Micah put it succinctly:

He has told you, O mortal, what is good;
and what does the LORD require of you
but to do justice, and to love kindness,
and to walk humbly with your God? (Micah 6:8)

6. THE CULTURAL SCENE AT COURT

The circumscribed interests of the author of the Book of Kings created many gaps in the narrative concerning life in ancient Judah; his focus on cult-related matters can easily lead to the misconception that little more than the Jerusalem Temple engaged Judah's king. But that was hardly the case. The extensive survey of the reign of King Solomon based upon excerpts from the "Book of the Acts of Solomon" (1 Kgs 10:41) shows otherwise. It is likely that this book, no longer extant, was composed by the circle of scholars and literati ("wise men") who served as advisors to Solomon. These elder statesmen depicted their king as an astute ruler in every aspect of government, from international relations (e.g., 1 Kgs 5:15–26; 10:1–13) to taxation and defense (1 Kgs 9:15–25), and even state-run commercial enterprises (1 Kgs 9:26–28; 10:26–29). Solomon was also a wise judge (1 Kgs 3:16–28), who excelled in didactic teaching:

> Solomon's wisdom surpassed the wisdom of all the people of the east, and all the wisdom of Egypt. He was wiser than anyone else, wiser than Ethan the Ezrahite, and Heman, Calcol, and Darda, children of Mahol; his fame spread throughout all the surrounding nations. He composed three thousand proverbs, and his songs numbered a thousand and five. He would speak of trees, from the cedar that is in the Lebanon to the hyssop that grows in the wall; he would speak of animals, and birds, and reptiles, and fish. People came from all the nations to hear the wisdom of Solomon; they came from all the kings of the earth who had heard of his wisdom.
>
> (1 Kgs 5:30–34 [Heb. 10–14])

This tradition carried over to the later collection of wisdom teaching in the Book of Proverbs that bears the title: "The proverbs of Solomon son of David, king of Israel" (Prov 1:1). Not all the proverbs in this book issued from the mouth of Solomon, as there are other authors mentioned in the book, e.g., Agur (Prov 30:1), Lemuel's mother (Prov 31:1).

The work of collection and edition of wisdom teachings was an ongoing literary activity, probably centered in the royal court. The preparation of one such collection is mentioned in Proverbs and credited to Hezekiah's men: "These too are proverbs of Solomon, which the men of King Hezekiah of Judah copied" (Prov 25:1). Royal sponsorship of this sort is not just a sign of the entrée this cohort of wise men enjoyed at court, but also of the ambience Hezekiah cultivated in the king's house.

Among the king's pleasures was music and song, but the music stopped following Judah's defeat in 701 BCE. Hezekiah had to part with his entertainers who were sent to Nineveh as part of the indemnity of surrender to Sennacherib.

> He, Hezekiah, was overwhelmed by the awesome splendor of my lordship, and he sent me after my departure to Nineveh, my royal city...his daughters, his palace women, his male and female singers....
>
> (see p. 23, Excursus 1)

These Judeans are immortalized on the walls of Sennacherib's palace, shown plucking their harps as they move along the road, goaded by an Assyrian soldier.

Judean musicians taken prisoner under escort by an Assyrian soldier (Courtesy of the Trustees of the British Museum).

7. THE KING'S NEAR-FATAL ILLNESS

It is rather unusual to hear of the health of a monarch, unless, of course, it affected the affairs of state, and even then the matter is reported in the briefest manner. Thus we learn that King Uzziah's leprosy caused him to withdraw from the daily affairs of state and take up residence in a sanatorium of sorts, passing on the reins to his son Jotham (2 Kgs 15:5). King Asa suffered from a foot ailment in his dotage (1 Kgs 15:23). Only with reference to Hezekiah's ailment[11] was a full account given:

> In those days Hezekiah became sick and was at the point of death. The prophet Isaiah son of Amoz came to him, and said to him, "Thus says the Lord: Set your house in order, for you shall die; you shall not recover." Then Hezekiah turned his face to the wall and prayed to the Lord: "Remember now, O Lord, I implore you, how I have walked before you in faithfulness with a whole heart, and have done what is good in your sight." Hezekiah wept bitterly. Before Isaiah had gone out of the middle court, the word of the Lord came to him: "Turn back, and say to Hezekiah prince of my people, Thus says the Lord, the God of your ancestor David: I have heard your prayer, I have seen your tears; indeed, I will heal you; on the third day you shall go up to the house of the Lord. I will add fifteen years to your life. I will deliver you and this city out of the hand of the king of Assyria; I will defend this city for my own sake and for my servant David's sake." Then Isaiah said, "Bring a lump of figs. Let them take it and apply it to the boil, so that he may recover." (2 Kgs 20:1–7)

It seems that Hezekiah's favored status brought the author of the Book of Kings to include this story in his survey of the king's rule. The tale points up a further side of Hezekiah's piety. His steadfast following the Lord stood in good stead; indeed it saved his life. Here, too, Isaiah's special relationship with the king is exhibited; the prophet served as intermediary between the king and his God, bringing messages of warning and comfort as the situation required. This medical crisis occurred midway in Hezekiah's reign as the remark "I will add fifteen years years to your life" makes clear – his total reign numbered 29 years (2 Kgs 18:2).

Apropos the king's illness, we learn that emissaries of the Babylonian king Merodach-baladan came to Jerusalem to inquire after the king's health (2 Kgs 20:12). Established protocol in the ancient Near East expected the exchange of greetings such as this, a sign of good diplomatic relations between rulers. Assyrian rulers considered it an affront, an act of great disrespect when a vassal king "did not send to inquire after my well-being." Regarding the meeting in Jerusalem, it is often suspected that more than a polite gesture was at hand. If the year was 713, as I suspect, the rebellion in Ashdod was in full swing and Hezekiah's display of his wealth and power to the Babylonians could be understood as a sign that he was ready for allied action against Assyria. But this is nowhere said, and other matters, for example, international trade, might also have been on the agenda.

8. THE KINGDOM OF JUDAH AS AN ASSYRIAN TRIBUTARY

For close to a quarter century, ever since ascending the throne in 727 BCE, Hezekiah succeeded in preserving the semi-independence of the kingdom of Judah vis-à-vis the Assyrian empire. Judah's status as a vassal had been initiated by his father Ahaz in response to the pressure by neighboring Samaria and Damascus to join an anti-Assyrian coalition (cf. 2 Kgs 16:7; Isa 7:1–9). Rather than risk the consequences of rebellion, Ahaz chose to submit to Tiglath-pileser III. Submission meant the payment of yearly tax and tribute, and maintaining political loyalty to Assyria, in particular, the forfeiture of an independent foreign policy. These onerous and confining requirements put Hezekiah's skill as a statesman to the test throughout his three decades on the throne, and more than once it appears that he was of two minds.

The monarchy in Assyria changed hands three times during the years of Hezekiah's rule: in the winter of 727/26, when Shalmaneser V took the throne on the death of Tiglath-pileser III; five years later, in the winter of 722/21, when Sargon II replaced Shalmaneser V; and in 705, when Sennacherib ascended the throne following Sargon's death. At each of these junctures many of Assyria's subjects rebelled to their eventual discomfiture. Therefore, it would not be in error to think that Hezekiah, like the others, faced the question of rebellion at times of transition in Assyria, weighing his chances for success against the powerful imperial forces. Unfortunately, the extant sources are minimal, leaving us only with speculation as to how Hezekiah navigated the ever-shifting political upheavals he encountered.

The first challenge to Hezekiah's Assyrian policy passed without incident. The year was 727, the year of his accession to the throne following the death of Ahaz; it was also the year in which Tiglath-pileser III died. The prophet Isaiah commented on the unrest that the demise of the Assyrian king had created in Philistia, and his words sent a clear message to his Judean audience:

> *In the year that King Ahaz died this oracle came:*
> *Do not rejoice, all you Philistines,*
> *that the rod that struck you is broken,*
> *for from the root of the snake will come forth an adder,*
> *and its fruit will be a flying fiery serpent.* (Isa 14:28–29)

Tiglath-pileser III's passing was not a time for celebration, for this snake that had bitten them will surely be followed by poisonous offspring! The message rang clear, and Hezekiah, a new and untried ruler, seems to have considered it prudent to remain submissive to Assyria, at least for the time being. The ensuing five-year reign of Shalmaneser V, which is for the most part undocumented, passed quietly for Judah. Hezekiah certainly took note of Samaria's failed attempt at rebellion against Assyria that led to the invasion and capture of the northern kingdom of Israel (cf. 2 Kgs 17:1–6; 18:9), and the lesson learnt was that the time was not ripe for rebellion.

The next moment of decision for Hezekiah occurred in the winter of 722/21, during which the unexpected death of Shalmaneser V destabilized Assyria both at home and abroad. Sargon II—apparently of royal blood, but not in the line of succession—seized the throne and fought to establish his rule in Assyria. Sargon faced strong internal opposition and he boasts of his gracious pardoning of "6,300 guilty Assyrians"—those who had opposed him. Rather than executing such a large group of native Assyrians, he had them resettled in northern Syria. In the south, Babylon broke away from Assyria and came under the rule of the Chaldean Merodach-baladan, and in the western reaches of the empire, rebellion had reached serious dimensions; under the leadership of Yau-bi'di of Hamath, provinces and vassal kingdoms rose up and "killed the citizens of Assyria who were present" in their region. Among the rebel areas, Sargon listed: Arpad, Ṣimirra, Damascus and Samaria; and there were others as well, for example, Gaza on the Philistine coast broke from Assyria and won the support of Shabaka, the Cushite ruler of Egypt, who sent armed forces to Philistia.

It is clear that retaking the West was vital for the continuation of the empire. In 720, after being forced into a military stalemate with Babylon, Sargon marched west. He overcame the insurgents in north and central Syria on the historic battlefield of Qarqar on the Orontes River, where in the mid-ninth century a western coalition had stopped Shalmaneser III's advance. Sargon deported Yau-bi'di of Hamath, his family and court to Assyria, where the rebel leader was summarily punished by flaying. By these moves, Assyria reasserted its hegemony over the northern territories.

During this western campaign of 720, the kingdom of Israel came to its final end. Though Samaria had been conquered by Shalmaneser V two years earlier, the death of the Assyrian king had halted the process of converting Samaria into an Assyrian province. Sargon seems to have won an easy victory, following which he deported 27,290 inhabitants from the territory of Samaria and brought foreign settlers to the newly established province of *Samerina* (Samaria).[12] A contingent of 200 Israelite charioteers were mobilized and attached to Sargon's personal guard (see *The Raging Torrent*, Text no. 5.02).

Throughout all this upheaval, nothing is heard of Judah

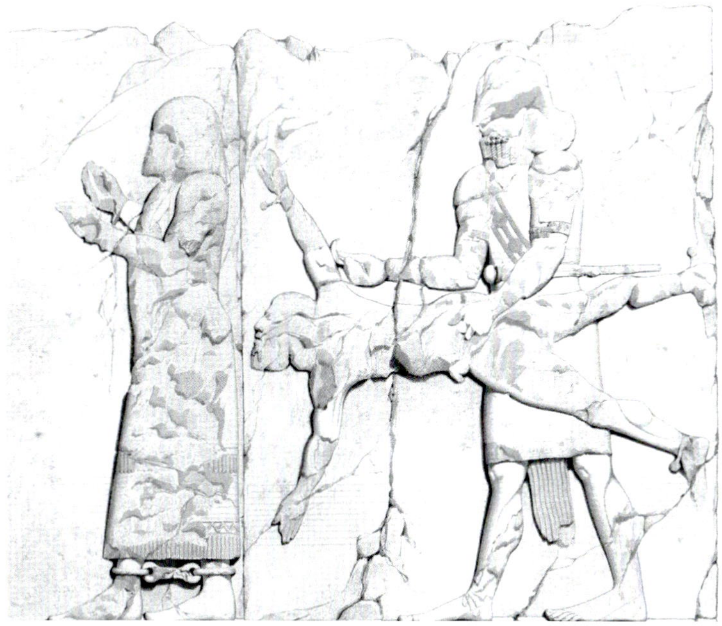

From a relief in the palace of Sargon II at Dur-Sharrukin (Khorsabad) with the epigraph: "I flayed Yau-bi'di of Hamath" (P. E. Botta–E. Flandin, *Monument de Ninive*, II, Paris 1849, Plate 120).

and whether it was a party to the insurrections. It may be that Hezekiah was a holdout, who chose caution rather than rebellion. Yet there is reason to suspect that this is not the full picture. To the north and to the west, Judah was surrounded by provinces and kingdoms in rebellion against Assyria. Besides, Sargon was not the designated heir to the throne and the transfer of loyalty to a usurper was not an established principle. With all due caution, one may suggest that Hezekiah was involved in the rebellion against Sargon at this juncture. In an inscription written in 717, three years after Sargon's western campaign, Sargon claims to being "the subduer of the land of Judah, whose place is far off" (*The Raging Torrent*, Text no. 5.07). For sure, the term "subduer" is equivocal; in Assyrian inscriptions it is used both for kingdoms who submitted after battle, as well as for those who choose to submit without a fight. In addition, though the text of Sargon's annal inscription is broken at this point in time, it has been suggested that the missing lines might have included a report on Judah's rebellion and some have even speculated what report these missing lines might have told us. Thus, while we cannot be sure, one should not rule out Hezekiah's complicity in the uprisings against Sargon. Whatever the case, for now, Judah did not suffer the devastating consequences that befell Samaria. Samaria had rebelled and lost; Judah continued on as an Assyrian vassal.

The next opportunity for Hezekiah to free Judah from its ties to Assyria came later in the same decade, during the rebellion against Sargon that broke out in Ashdod in 713–712. Judah was implicated in the surreptitious negotiations led by Yamani of Ashdod who sought to build a southern coalition opposed to Assyrian heavy-handed supervision of the coastal trade in Philistia. An annalistic text from Nineveh reports:

> (They [the Ashdodites] sent) seditious words and slander to the k[ings] of Philistia, Judah, Ed[om,] Moab, (and) the residents of the sea(coast), who bear the tax and gifts of the god Ashur, my lord, to make them hostile towards me. They sent bribes to Pharaoh, king of Egypt, a king who cannot save them, to seek his aid. (*The Raging Torrent*, Text No. 5.08).

Again, though it is nowhere stated that Hezekiah supported this move, a fragmentary Assyrian text, which resembles a composition known as Sargon's "Letter to the god Ashur," reports on the attack against the Judean fortress of Azekah during Hezekiah's reign (*The Raging Torrent*, Text No. 5.10). If this text is indeed dated to the reign of Sargon, as it looks, then it may be related to the Assyrian campaign in 712; it attests to the fact that Hezekiah had indeed been a partner to the Ashdod rebellion, and as a result, he suffered the loss of a major city in the Shephelah that likely forced him to surrender, just in time to save Judah from further punishment.

These losses should have been a lesson for Hezekiah concerning Assyria's seriousness with regard to control of the trade routes that ran through the Land of Israel; yet it seems that it was a lesson only partially learnt. For as it turned out, Judah's king did not give up all thought of freeing himself from tax and tribute payments. Less than a decade later, Judah was again in a state of rebellion, this time with Hezekiah as the ostensive head of an area-wide uprising (see below).

9. THE REBELLION AGAINST ASSYRIA IN 705–701 BCE

The Background

The year 705 was a fateful year for Assyria and all those who were subject to the empire. During an Assyrian campaign to Anatolia, Sargon was killed in battle in Tabal; his death and the fact that his body was not recovered suggested to many in the empire that Assyria's power had weakened.[13] The circumstances seemed right to throw off vassal bonds. In the west, Hezekiah, together with other neighboring kingdoms—among them Tyre, Ashkelon and Ekron—withheld recognition of Sennacherib, Sargon's son and heir. And at first, this seditious step must have looked like it would succeed, for it took Sennacherib four years to mount a campaign to regain control of the Mediterranean coast and the Land of Israel. This he did in 701 BCE.

Preparations for War

The intervening years between 705 and 701 were well spent by the rebels as they prepared the defense of their lands in advance of the anticipated return of the Assyrian army. A united front was sought, and to this end, Hezekiah, the leading figure among the anti-Assyrians, moved with force against some of the Philistine kingdoms on the southern coast – "He smote the Philistines as far as Gaza and its territory, from

A royal dedicatory inscription on stone from the temple of the goddess PTGYH, "queen of Ekron," built by Akayus/Ikausu, son of Padi, king of Ekron; early seventh century BCE (on display at the Israel Museum; photo Oren Rozen, via Wikimedia Commons).

Remains of the Broad Wall today in the Jewish Quarter (photo Ian Scott, via Wikimedia Commons)

watchtower to fortified city" (2 Kgs 18:8) – no doubt because they were hesitant or were opposed to the war. Hezekiah's assertive actions are exemplified by his involvement in the internal politics of the Philistine city of Ekron (Tel Miqne). The city's leaders had taken a stand in support of resisting Assyria; they ousted their pro-Assyrian king, Padi, and handed him over to Hezekiah, who imprisoned him in Jerusalem (so according to Sennacherib's account; see p. 23). They were active in securing foreign support for the rebel cause, in particular, from Shabatka, the Cushite ruler of Egypt. Judah, too, took part in the negotiations with its powerful southern neighbor.

But not everyone applauded these moves. Isaiah typically inveighed against "those who go down to Egypt for help and rely on horses, who trust in chariots because they are many, and on horsemen because they are very strong." His cry against those who "do not look to the Holy One of Israel or consult the LORD!" (Isa 31:1) was consistent with the stance he had taken in years previous against such foreign entanglements.

As noted earlier, during the first decade of Sargon's reign, relations between Egypt and Assyria had stabilized and remained quiescent as result of Sargon's two-pronged Assyrian policy in Philistia: the stationing of an Assyrian military presence at the northern border of the Sinai Peninsula at Raphiah (*The Raging Torrent*, Text no. 5.01, lines 23–27), and the fostering of an open trade zone in this area between Egypt and Assyria (*The Raging Torrent*, Text no. 5.02). But when Sargon died, Shabatka changed course and sent military units to aid the rebels. Sennacherib's account tells of a major battle between the Assyrian army and an Egyptian force at Eltekeh (see below).

A major facet of Judah's preparedness was the physical strengthening of the fortifications of the realm and the laying in of stores ahead of siege and battle. Again, Isaiah, the always critical witness to what he considered the godless activities of Judah's leaders, tells of the intensive construction undertaken in the capital at this time of crisis:

> On that day you looked to the weapons of the House of the Forest, and you saw that there were many breaches in the city of David, and you collected the waters of the lower pool. You counted the houses of Jerusalem, and you broke down the houses to fortify the wall. You made a reservoir between the two walls for the water of the old pool. But you did not look to him who did it, or have regard for him who planned it long ago. (Isa 22:8–11)

The three concerns to which the prophet referred were not unusual for a city that anticipated an attack or a long siege: the store of weapons, the reinforcement of the city wall and the insuring of a ready supply of water.

Archaeological excavations in the walled city of Jerusalem have elucidated two aspects of Isaiah's description. On the western hill, the so-called Upper City—today's Jewish Quarter—a suburban residential area had developed beginning in the ninth century BCE; within this locality a section of a massive wall, 65 meters long and 7 meters thick, of both finished and unfinished stone, has been uncovered. This city wall can be dated to the end of the eigth century and was surely meant to protect this extra-mural quarter from attack. In several places the wall was laid atop earlier constructions,

JERUSALEM AT THE TIME OF HEZEKIAH

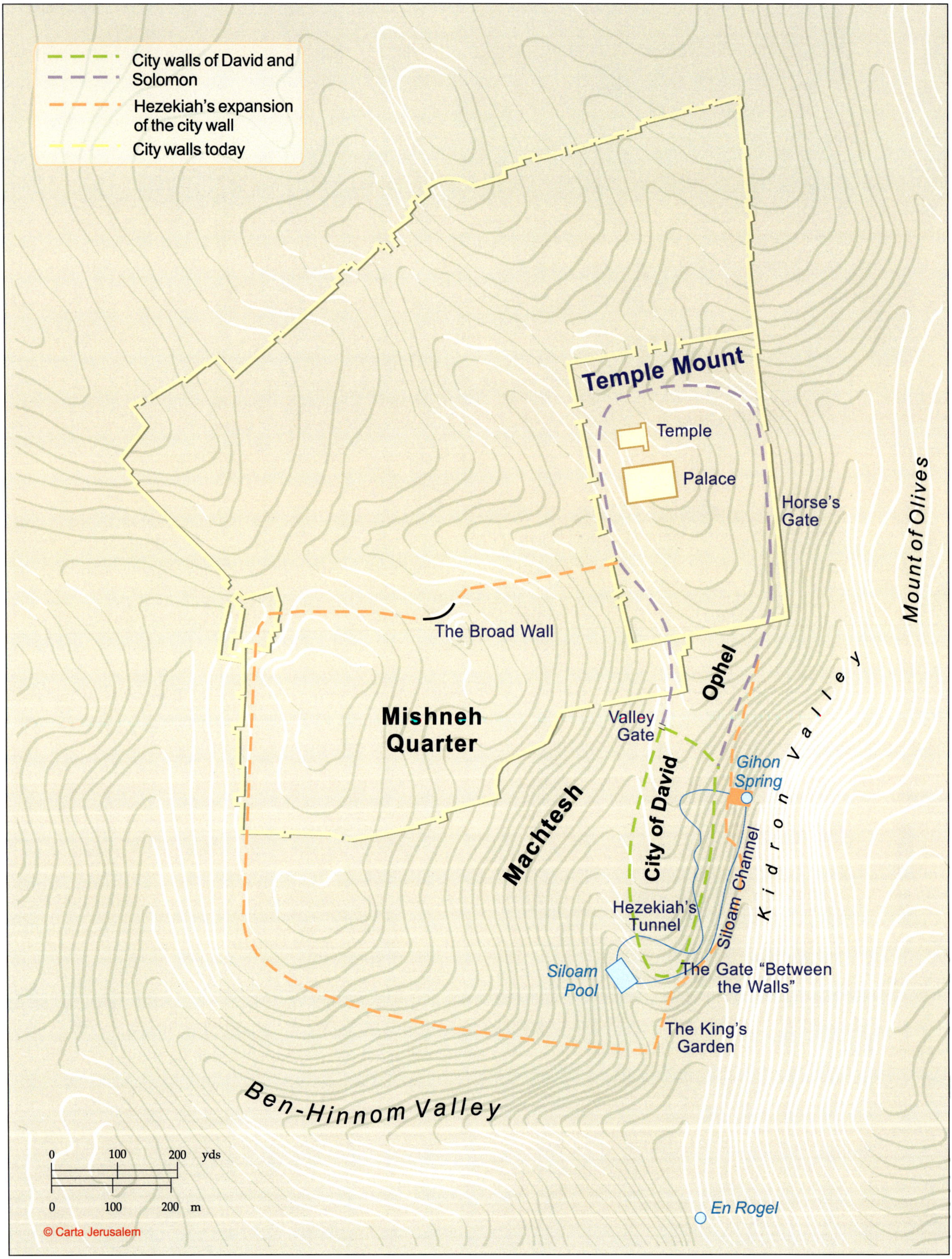

Interior of Hezekiah's Tunnel (photo: Tamar Hayardeni, via Wikimedia Commons).

explicating Isaiah's description of tearing down old structures in favor of the new defenses. The line of this "Broad Wall" (after the name of the wall as given in Neh 3:8) seems to have run west from the Temple Mount to the Hinnom Valley and then south, following the Hinnom east to its conjuncture with the Kidron Valley at the southeastern corner of the City of David.

As to Jerusalem's water supply, Hezekiah is credited with several hydraulic projects aimed at providing water to a growing city. A short notice in the Book of Kings relates that "he made the pool and the conduit and brought water into the city" (2 Kgs 20:20). The location and the circumstances of this work were apparently so well known that the author did not find it necessary to give further details. These were supplied by the early modern investigators of the town, who discovered the conduit in the Kidron Valley by the Gihon Spring, at the foot of the eastern wall of the City of David, from which over 1,500 cubic meters of water issue daily. In the second millennium BCE, a series of tunnels had been dug through the hillside; a vertical pier ("Warren's Shaft") led down to the spring, permitting the town's dwellers to draw water from within the city without having to climb down outside the city's defenses. In addition, at the mouth of the spring the excavators found the opening of a meandering tunnel that runs 533 m under the hill of the City of David from the Gihon to the Siloam Pool at the southern end of the city. The nature of the construction dates the tunnel to the eighth century BCE (Iron Age II), which confirms its association with Hezekiah.

At about 6 m before the tunnel reaches the pool, a six-line Hebrew inscription in elegant monumental script was incised on the wall, describing the method of excavation.

> While [ ] (were) still [ ] the axe(s) toward one another, and while there were still three cubits to be [tunneled, there was heard] a voice calling to his fellow, for there was a fissure(?) in the rock on the right [and on the left]. And on the day when the tunnel was cut through, the stonecutters struck toward one another, ax against ax. The water flowed from the source to the pool for 1,200 cubits, and the height of the rock was 100 cubits above the heads of the stonecutters.

Concerning the engineering aspects of the excavation, it may be that the two teams were following a natural fissure in the karstic rock through which water seeped as a guide.[14]

A second water project connected with the Gihon was meant specifically to be a defensive measure. It is reported by the later biblical Chronicler:

> After these things and these acts of faithfulness, King Sennacherib of Assyria came and invaded Judah and encamped against the fortified cities, thinking to win them for himself. When Hezekiah saw that Sennacherib had come and intended to fight against Jerusalem, he planned with

The course of Hezekiah's Tunnel.

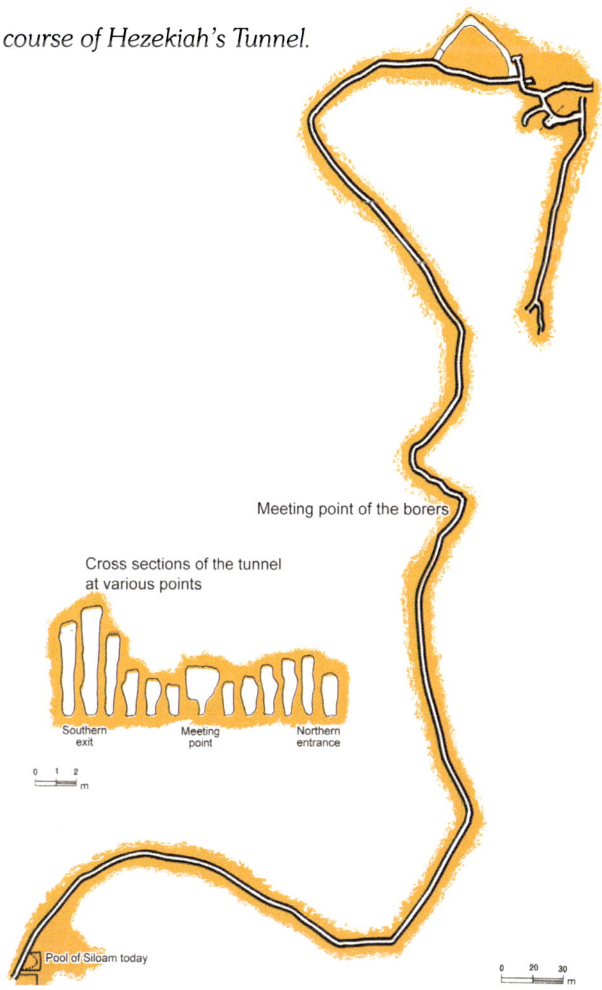

(right, above) The Siloam Inscription (now in the Museum of Ancient Near Eastern Antiquities, Istanbul) *and facsimile* (Ada Yardeni).

> his officers and his warriors to stop the flow of the springs that were outside the city; and they helped him. A great many people were gathered, and they stopped all the springs and the wadi that flowed through the land, saying, "Why should the Assyrian kings come and find water in abundance?" (2 Chron 32:1–4)

The reference here seems to be to the Siloam Channel II that runs above the foot of the Kidron Valley, which is part open, and part covered. This channel carried overflow water from the Gihon Spring to the agricultural plots in the valley ("The King's Garden"; 2 Kgs 25:4) and ended at the "Lower Pool" (Isa 22:9; Birket el-Hamrah). It was found blocked by large stones, perhaps evidence of Hezekiah's activity prior to the war.

The Course of the War

The Sources—A Critical Presentation

Reconstructing the course of the war in 701 BCE is a daunting challenge, given the relatively large number of sources that relate to it. Complementing the written biblical and Assyrian accounts are the rich material finds from archaeological excavations throughout the kingdom of Judah. But even when these witnesses touch upon the same events, they treat them in a tendentious manner, giving deference to the interests of their authors and their audience. These discrete perspectives give rise to several conundrums.

I. Biblical accounts

The biblical witnesses to the events of 701 are assembled in 2 Kings 18:13–19:37, and most of this text also appears in the Book of Isaiah (Isa 36–37) as an appendix to the main collection of his prophecies.[15] The reports given in Second Kings were reinterpreted some 200 years later in the Persian period and are given in the Book of Chronicles (2 Chron 32).

Critics have identified three separate accounts in 2 Kings 18–19; the first one is independent of the other two, which are related to each other as explained below.[16]

Account 1 (often referred to as the "A" account): 2 Kgs 18:13–16.
This four-verse unit, utilizing several chronistic notes, summarizes the opening and closing stages of Sennacherib's attack on Judah, without any reference to Jerusalem or the negotiations between the sides. They report that the Assyrian king succeeded in conquering all the fortified cities of the land, whereupon Hezekiah sued for surrender and delivered the agreed-upon payment of a heavy indemnity to the Assyrian king encamped at Lachish.

Account 2 (often referred to as "B1"): 2 Kgs 18:17–19:9a, 36–37.
This is a prophetic tale (so named because of the role played by Isaiah) that shows acquaintance with specific realistic details, suggesting that it was drawn up a generation or two after the events of 701 BCE. The focus of this tale is the speech of the Rabshakeh at the walls of Jerusalem, during which this Assyrian high official delivers a demand for surrender to the representatives of King Hezekiah. He explains, within earshot of the defenders on the city walls, that Assyria's army is invincible, and Judah's trust in Egypt will prove to be a disappointment. And besides, claimed the Rabshakeh, Assyria has moved against Judah with the support of the Lord, Israel's God. Surrender and exile would be the wisest course to follow. Upon hearing this message, the frightened Judean king turns to Isaiah and asks that he pray to his God for salvation. Isaiah promises Hezekiah that Sennacherib will retreat and, as punishment for his blasphemies, he will be murdered, a promise that in this account is indeed fulfilled.

Account 3 (often referred to as "B2"): 2 Kgs 19:9b–35.
This is a second prophetic tale that follows the outline of the first one, a sign of its acquaintance with it, but departs from it due to significant ideological development; B2 likely reached its present form about a century after the events, towards the end of the seventh century BCE. In this telling, Hezekiah personally received a written message from Sennacherib demanding his surrender, in response to which, Hezekiah ascended to the Temple to pray to the Lord for rescue. Isaiah appeared to deliver the Lord's message of encouragement. His words included a lengthy prophetic harangue against the Assyrian king and a prediction of his withdrawal, thus

Translation of Sennacherib's Third Campaign as inscribed on the Rassam Cylinder

32–35 In my third campaign, I marched to Ḫatti. The awesome splendor of my lordship overwhelmed Luli, king of Sidon, and he fled overseas far-off. The terrifying nature of the weapon of (the god) Ashur my lord overwhelmed his strong cities, Greater Sidon, Little Sidon, Bit-zitti, Ṣariptu, Maḫaliba, Ushu, Achzib, Acco, walled cities (provided) with food and water for his garrisons, and they bowed in submission at my feet. I installed Tubaʾlu on his royal throne over them and imposed upon him tribute and dues for my lordship (payable) annually without interruption.

36–38 The kings of Amurru, all of them—Minuḫimmu of Samsimuruna, Tubaʾlu of Sidon, Abdiliʾti of Arvad, Urumilki of Byblos, Mitinti of Ashdod, Puduʾilu of Beth-Ammon, Chemosh-nadbi of Moab, Ayarammu of Edom—brought me sumptuous presents as their abundant audience-gift, fourfold, and kissed my feet.

39–41 As for Ṣidqa, king of Ashkelon, who had not submitted to my yoke—his family gods, he himself, his wife, his sons, his daughters, his brothers, and (all the rest of) his descendants, I deported and brought him to Assyria. I set Sharru-lu-dari, son of Rukibti, their former king, over the people of Ashkelon and imposed upon him payment of tribute (and) presents to my lordship; he (now) bears my yoke. In the course of my campaign, I surrounded and conquered Beth-Dagon, Joppa, Bene-berak, Azor, cities belonging to Ṣidqa, who did not submit quickly, and I carried off their spoil.

42–48 The officials, the nobles, and the people of Ekron who had thrown Padi, their king, (who was) under oath and obligation to Assyria, into iron fetters and handed him over in a hostile manner to Hezekiah, the Judean, took fright because of the offense they had committed. The kings of Egypt, (and) the bowmen, chariot corps and cavalry of the king of Cush assembled a countless force and came to their (i.e., the Ekronites) aid. In the plain of Eltekeh, they drew up their ranks against me and sharpened their weapons. Trusting in the god Ashur, my lord, I fought with them and inflicted a defeat upon them. The Egyptian charioteers and princes, together with the charioteers of the Cushites, I personally took alive in the midst of the battle. I besieged and conquered Eltekeh and Timnah and carried off their spoil. I advanced to Ekron and slew its officials and nobles who had stirred up rebellion and hung their bodies on watchtowers all about the city. The citizens who committed sinful acts, I counted as spoil, and I ordered the release of the rest of them, who had not sinned. I freed Padi, their king, from Jerusalem and set him on the throne as king over them and imposed tribute for my lordship over him.

49–54 As for Hezekiah, the Judean, I besieged 46 of his fortified walled cities and surrounding smaller towns, which were without number. Using packed-down ramps and applying battering rams, infantry attacks by mines, breeches, and siege machines (or perhaps: storm ladders), I conquered (them). I took out 200,150 people, young and old, male and female, horses, mules, donkeys, camels, cattle, and sheep, without number, and counted them as spoil. He himself, I locked up within Jerusalem, his royal city, like a bird in a cage. I surrounded him with armed posts, and made it unthinkable (literally, "taboo") for him to exit by the city gate. His cities which I had despoiled, I cut off from his land and gave them to Mitinti, king of Ashdod, Padi, king of Ekron, and Ṣilli-Bel, king of Gaza, and thus diminished his land. I imposed dues and gifts for my lordship upon him, in addition to the former tribute, their yearly payment.

55–58 He, Hezekiah, was overwhelmed by the awesome splendor of my lordship, and he sent me after my departure to Nineveh, my royal city, his elite troops (and) his best soldiers, which he had brought in as reinforcements to strengthen Jerusalem, his royal city, with 30 talents of gold, 800 talents of silver, choice antimony, large blocks of carnelian, beds (inlaid) with ivory, armchairs (inlaid) with ivory, elephant hides, ivory, ebony-wood, boxwood, multicolored garments, garments of linen, wool (dyed) red-purple and blue-purple, vessels of copper, iron, bronze and tin, iron, chariots, siege shields, lances, armor, daggers for the belt, bows and arrows, countless trappings and implements of war, together with his daughters, his palace women, his male and female singers. He (also) dispatched his messenger to deliver the tribute and to do obeisance.

(*The Raging Torrent*, Text no. 6.01)

Rassam Cylinder (Courtesy of the Trustees of the British Museum).

SENNACHERIB'S CAMPAIGN TO THE WEST, 701 BCE

protecting Jerusalem and the House of David from attack. In fulfillment of this prediction, that very night the angel of the Lord slew 185,000 Assyrian soldiers, following which Sennacherib abandoned his plan to attack Jerusalem.

These three accounts are not consecutive, and in certain points, they appear to contradict one another. For example, neither of the two prophetic tales relates to the preceding statement that told of Hezekiah's surrender and his payment of a large indemnity to Sennacherib (2 Kgs 18:14–16). On the other hand, the two prophetic tales both end with a victory for Hezekiah; in the first one, Sennacherib returns home to meet his death at the hands of his sons (19:37); in the second one, he withdraws after a massive slaughter of the Assyrian forces (19:35). It was the author-editor of the Book of Kings who edited and arranged the three accounts so that his audience would understand the special place held by Jerusalem as the Lord's city. The payment made by Hezekiah to Sennacherib was of minor importance and it was given short shrift; not so the verbal attack by Sennacherib against the Lord and his intention to attack Jerusalem. Because Jerusalem was a city under divine protection, the manner of its salvation was set out in full.

II. The Assyrian account

The annals of Sennacherib report in full outline the Assyrian king's "third (military) campaign" undertaken in 701 BCE. The text, known as the Rassam cylinder, after its discoverer, Hormuzd Rassam, was written in Spring, 700 BCE, just months after the close of the campaign (see p. 23).[17] Its description is suffused with expressions of Assyrian royal ideology, particularly the claim of total victory over all of Assyria's enemies in the West. Concerning Judah, the annals tell of the capture of 46 cities and smaller settlements, the deportation of over 200,000 persons, and an onerous siege laid against Jerusalem. Hezekiah was locked up "like a bird in a cage," and had no choice but to surrender. Contrite and repentant, Hezekiah sent a vast tribute to Sennacherib delivered in Nineveh.

On the basis of a critical reading of these accounts, the following reconstruction of the events in 701 is presented. A word of caution is in place: even though the Assyrian annal account is a literary ideological document, it is the only report that gives some information on the military engagements of the Assyrian army with the western rebels, and so is used here as a guide for reconstructing the movements of the army.

Stage One: The Phoenician Kingdoms

The start of the campaign is not indicated, but the muster of the army and its movement west likely took place in early spring, with the passing of the winter rains, as was the practice in similar circumstances. Once it had reached the Mediterranean, the Assyrian army proceeded south along the coast, and at each stage on the way, Sennacherib received gifts from a number of north Phoenician kings who renewed their pledge of loyalty: Minuḫimmu of Samsimuruna, Abdili'ti of Arvad, and Urumilki of Byblos. At Sidon (40 km south of Beirut), he encountered the first of the rebels, Luli, king of Sidon and Tyre (i.e., Eloulaios, in Josephus, *Antiquities*, 9.283). His kingdom extended from Sidon southwards to Acco, as far as Mount Carmel. Luli had maneuvered for decades between independence and submission to Assyria; overseas he fought and maintained the Phoenician presence on the island of Cyprus. However, contrary to his expectations, his forces were no match for the Assyrian army and they submitted, it seems, without much of a battle. Luli chose to abandon his fortress on Tyre, the island city about 1 km from the coast, and fled to Cyprus, where he died five years later. Sennacherib reorganized the political order in the area; Sidon became the center of the kingdom, now free of Tyre, and Tuba'lu was set on the throne. Because Assyria had no navy of its own, Tyre could not be captured, but it was divested of much of its coastal holdings. Captives "from the land of Tyre" were deported to Assyria where they "made bricks" and "hauled reeds" for the reconstruction of the temples and palaces of Nineveh, the pride of Sennacherib's civic projects (see *The Raging Torrent*, Text no. 6.04).

(left) Assyrian slingers and archers at the city of Lachish; and (below), pile of flint stones found at Lachish, evidence of battle. (Courtesy of the Trustees of the British Museum)

Stage Two: The Philistine Kingdoms

The Assyrian army continued its march southward towards the Philistine kingdoms, passing by the port city of Dor on its way through the territory of the province of *Samerina* (i.e., Samaria). At Assyrian-controlled cities such as Dor, the local administration supplied needed provisions to the troops on campaign.

The first encounter in Philistia was with the kingdom of Ashkelon, which under its king, Ṣidqa, dominated areas north of the city up to the Yarkon River. The cities in this enclave—Beth-dagon, Joppa, Bene-berak, Azor—were captured and despoiled. From there, the army continued south to Ashkelon. It is not clear whether a battle over the city ensued; the annals do not report one. It could be that the early losses had weakened the city's defenses, and as a result Ashkelon put up minimal resistance and fell easily. Sennacherib reports that he carried off as prisoners to Assyria: Ṣidqa, his family and court, as well as the images of his ancestral gods. Ashkelon's new ruler, installed by Sennacherib, was Sharru-lu-dari, the son of a former king, Rukubiti, who had pledged his loyalty to Assyria a quarter century earlier during the days of Tiglath-pileser III (see *The Raging Torrent*, Text no. 4.10); it is likely that Rukubti had been ousted (or killed?) by those who supported the anti-Assyrian Ṣidqa. Rukubti's son, Sharru-lu-dari, bore an Assyrian name—it means: "May the king live forever"—which suggests that he had likely spent time at the Assyrian court as hostage for his father's continued loyalty. Now, considering that he had been re-educated in Assyrian ways, he could be trusted to occupy his father's throne as an Assyrian client.

The two other major Philistine cities on the coast, Ashdod and Gaza, are not mentioned in the Assyrian record as having joined the other kingdoms in the rebellion; yet it is hard to imagine that they were able to sit on the sidelines as their belligerent neighbors prepared for battle. The policies of both cities may have been driven by outside pressures. For one, Gaza. It is reported that Hezekiah had "attacked the Philistines as far as Gaza and its territory, from watchtower to fortified city" (2 Kgs 18:8), a move no doubt prompted by the city's strategic location at the eastern exit of the road that ran along the coast of the north Sinai Peninsula connecting Egypt and Philistia. During the second millennium BCE, Gaza often served as the staging ground for Egyptian forces as they entered Canaan on their way to military engagements. Now, at the end of the eighth century, when the Cushite-Egyptian forces came to support the anti-Assyrian rebels (see below), it would likely have looked to Gaza to serve as the base of operations and so it was important for Hezekiah to neutralize potential resistance by local pro-Assyrian groups in the area. As to Ashdod, its location north of Ashkelon would have exposed the city to Ṣidqa's hostile moves. Yet there is no explicit evidence on the fate of either city during the battles. The Assyrian annals do mention that at the war's end, Sennacherib transferred the administration of large tracts of captured Judean territory to both Gaza and Ashdod, an arrangement that probably lasted well into the seventh century. These gifts of land strongly suggest that they had aligned themselves with Assyria.

The inland Philistine city of Ekron in the northern Shephelah did not fare better than its neighbors. Ekron's city leaders had opted to join Hezekiah in rebellion, going back on the pro-Assyrian policy of their king Padi. Padi was removed and incarcerated in Jerusalem for the duration of the war. The Ekronites were active in securing Egyptian support for the rebel cause, but the Egyptian interlude only delayed the Assyrian attack and capture of the city. Sennacherib boasts of how he dealt with the rebels of Ekron—"I slew its officials and nobles who had stirred up rebellion and hung their bodies on watchtowers all about the city." Similar punitive action is depicted on the Lachish relief, where we see a number of Lachishites impaled in front of the city's walls (see image below). To us moderns, these actions have all the earmarks of cruel and unusual punishment. But these scenes at Lachish and Ekron were not at all unusual. On the contrary, impaling was a regular part of Assyrian military operations. The gruesome display of the executed around a captured city was meant to put the fear of Assyria into the hearts of the defeated. There was obviously no concern among the Assyrians that this object lesson would earn them a reputation among modern historians as being a particularly brutal folk.

Impalement at Lachish; detail of relief from Sennacherib's Southwest Palace at Nineveh (Courtesy of the Trustees of the British Museum).

Stage 3: The Egyptian Interlude

According to the Assyrian report, an Egyptian force made up of native Egyptians from the Delta and Cushites from Upper Egypt met Sennacherib at Eltekeh (possibly Tell esh-Shallaf, about 3 km west of the city of Rehoboth) on the coastal plain. They were led by Tirhakah, a young man, twenty years of age, who had been called by his brother Shabatka, the Cushite king of Egypt, to join him. Tirhakah (in Egyptian: Taharqa) would take the throne of Egypt a decade later (reigning from 690–664 BCE), and it is by the title "king of Egypt" that he is referred to in the first prophetic tale (2 Kgs 19:9).

The point in time of the battle at Eltekeh cannot be determined, as the timeline of most of the engagements of 701 remains surmise. Following the arduous crossing of the northern Sinai and its bivouac at Gaza, the Egyptian army likely moved to positions north of Ashkelon ahead of the Assyrian advance. Egyptian units also reinforced local troops located at key rebel cities, for example, Lachish; this is evidenced by the depiction of the execution of Cushite soldiers after the fall of the city. Thus, it seems likely that the Assyrian forces were met by the main Egyptian army as they moved south to the Philistine heartland after taking the Ashkelon enclave. Sennacherib claimed victory over the Egyptians at Eltekeh and that he personally captured Cushite charioteers alive in the midst of battle; both of these boasts are typical of Assyrian reporting. For the present, this remains the only evidence of this engagement. The singular reference to Tirhakah in 2 Kgs 19:9 is of no help whatsoever in this regard. Minimally speaking, the Egyptians had made their showing and were thrown back; for the Assyrians the way had been cleared to continue on to Ashkelon on the coast and then to Ekron and the Judean fortresses in the Shephelah. They had no interest in pursuing the Egyptians or in advancing beyond the Gaza–Raphiah march.

Stage 4: The Kingdom of Judah

There is little doubt that Hezekiah of Judah was seen as the major opponent to Assyrian interests, the instigator and leader of the rebel camp. In somewhat later inscriptions, the Assyrian scribes spoke of him as "stubborn and mighty." More space was given over in the Assyrian annals to describing the battles in Judah than to any other engagement. The claim that "46 of his (Hezekiah's) fortified walled cities and surrounding small towns" fell to the mighty attacks of the Assyrian army complements the report in 2 Kings 18 that "King Sennacherib of Assyria came up against all the fortified cities of Judah and captured them" (18:13). But none of these towns and villages are named. Levels of the destruction at many sites in Judah have been dated archaeologically to the end of the eighth century BCE and can safely be associated with the war in 701 BCE. Isaiah's testimony attests to the ruin on all fronts (save Jerusalem):

Your country lies desolate,
your cities are burned with fire;
in your very presence
aliens devour your land;
it is desolate, as overthrown by foreigners.
And daughter Zion is left
like a booth in a vineyard,
like a shelter in a cucumber field,
like a besieged city.
If the LORD of hosts
had not left us a few survivors,

The walls of Lachish and the road leading to the city's main gate (photo Oren Peles, via Wikimedia Commons).

we would have been like Sodom,
and become like Gomorrah. (Isa 1:7–9)

The congruence of all these reports leaves little doubt that the kingdom of Judah was a devastated land at the end of the hostilities.

The Battle at the City of Lachish

The names of the defeated and destroyed Judean cities are not given in any of the extant Assyrian accounts. The one exception is the reference to Jerusalem, the Judean capital, that came under heavy siege. The cities of Lachish and Libnah are mentioned as the sites of battles in 2 Kgs 18:14; 19:8. As luck would have it, these minimal references are upstaged by the pictorial presentation of the conquest of Lachish that once decorated the walls of an inner chamber in Sennacherib's palace at Nineveh.

Lachish was the largest of the Judean fortresses in the Shephelah, the undulating hill country that rises from the low-lying coastal plain through which the roads that lead up to the Judean mountains pass. Lachish stood at the southern end of the north-south string of fortresses (Beth-shemesh, Azekah, Libnah, Lachish), well-armed and well-stocked, on guard against the Assyrian invader.

Sennacherib set up his main camp at this strategic site, from which he personally oversaw the battle and its victory. This seems to explain the choice of Lachish for display in Sennacherib's "Palace without Rival"; the conquest of Lachish was the apex of his military achievements in 701.

Excavations at Lachish

Two major excavations have been carried out at Lachish; the first one by the British Wellcome–Marston Expedition in 1932–38, and the second by the Tel Aviv University Excavations in 1974–87. The history of settlement at the site, reaching back to prehistoric periods down to the Hellenistic Age, confirms the importance of Lachish throughout time. Concerning Sennacherib's campaign, the archaeologist's spade has clarified many aspects of the battle waged by the Assyrians to take the city.

The eighth-century occupation level (Level III) shows signs of strengthening the city's fortifications, perhaps associated with the preparations of the expected war with Assyria. Evidence of the Assyrian attack was found in the debris of Level III—arrowheads, the remnant of a soldier's helmet, a lengthy piece of an iron chain. Most prominent were the remains of the Assyrian siege ramp built at the southwestern corner of the tel. For the first time, a ramp of this sort was studied by the Tel Aviv team. Excavation clarified its size and structure, and helped in understanding the immense effort expended the construction. Between 13,000 and 19,000 tons

Two Assyrian scribes listing the fallen during battle. Detail of relief from the palace of Sennacherib at Nineveh (Courtesy of the Trustees of the British Museum).

A Judean family, with possesstions on wagon, leaving Lachish on the way to exile; detail of relief from Sennacherib's Southwest Palace at Nineveh (Courtesy of the Trustees of the British Museum).

of field rock and dirt were heaped up in the fan-like ramp. The defenders of Lachish were not oblivious to the Assyrian plan and prepared for the worst. They built a counter-ramp within the city opposite the ramp being built outside, which would have allowed them to make a stand against the invaders at the level of the anticipated breakthrough of the city's defensive wall.

The Lachish Relief

The artist who prepared the wall relief could have learned of the battle from a written source, a campaign itinerary of sorts kept by the scribes who were part of the army staff (though it must be admitted that such first-hand documents have not survived). Some have speculated that the artist was on hand at Lachish where he made sketches of the site and the stages of the battle, which he later consulted while preparing the relief.

The relief is a montage that superimposes a large number of operations upon one another that in actuality took place over time. Thus, the viewer sees the ongoing battle at the city walls, and at the same time, observes a line of refugees exiting the city gate from where they are led in submissive review before the victorious Sennacherib, who is shown seated on his throne at the near-by camp. The written description of the methods of attack of the Assyrian army in the annal report—"using

(above) The Lachish relief, from Sennacherib's Southwest Palace at Nineveh (Courtesy of the Trustees of the British Museum) *and (left) drawing* (from D. Ussishkin, *The Conquest of Lachish by Sennacherib*, Tel Aviv 1982).

packed down ramps and applying battering rams, infantry attacks by mines, breeches, and siege machines (or perhaps: storm ladders)"—is on full display in the relief. Of interest is the siege ramp that had been built against the walls of Lachish that served the forces who brought up military equipment within close range of the city. From there, the siege machines could apply their battering rams to the city wall and its gate. Archers approach behind the cover of full-body shields. Above the attackers, one sees the city's defenders pushing back the enemy ladders and their climbers, while other Lachishites throw stones and torches down on the Assyrian troops, who had prepared for this move; the siege machines are shown to have been equipped with a fire-fighting mechanism, a primitive extinguisher is seen in operation (see outline on image, p. 29).

The artist of the relief did not spare the viewer a taste of the brutal punishments meted out to the rebels; in fact, their display was one of the objectives of the relief. Not only were such acts meant as a warning for the survivors of the battle, they also aimed to impress guests and visitors to Sennacherib's palace with Assyria's power and determination to rule. Thus, the bodies of the dead are shown impaled on posts around walls of Lachish. Cushite soldiers, who had come to reenforce the local Judean troops, appear sprawled on the ground, as their skin is stripped away. The expression "calculated frightfulness" has been coined for such acts and it surely seems that the Assyrian army was well trained in cruel behavior.

The residents of Lachish who survived the battle can be seen leaving the city on their way to exile. This representation is the earliest picture of Judeans, an ancient "photograph" of sorts, giving invaluable information on their dress and their personal goods. Entire families had packed what could be carried by hand or loaded on a ox-drawn cart, the minimal necessities for the long trip to Assyria.

Negotiations for the Surrender at Jerusalem

As Assyria continued to pile up victories against the western kingdoms that had allied against Assyria, Sennacherib turned to Judah, and in what may seem to be a surprising move, he opened a window to negotiations with Hezekiah over terms of surrender. Now negotiation with an enemy should not be understood as a sign of incapacity or fatigue, certainly not when initiated by the Assyrians; it was a tactic aimed at conserving forces, and at the same time, sought to weaken the enemy by raising doubts about the wisdom of continued resistance. Sennacherib's predecessors had used it a number of times. For example, a representative of Tiglath-pileser III dealt with "the citizens of Babylon in front of the (city) gate" and offered them a remission of taxes if they would give up hostilities (*Bound for Exile*, no. 4.02). Similarly, during Sargon's Median wars, an Assyrian officer is known to have offered terms to the defenders of the embattled city of Pazashi (see below). The appearance of the Rabshakeh before the walls of Jerusalem dealing with the Judean delegation is of similar character. Coming to terms held advantages to both sides.

It is told that Rabshakeh and company arrived with "a great army" (2 Kgs 18:17), which may mean their siege of Jerusalem was underway. The description in the annal text could be referring to this stage in the war when it reports:

> He himself, I locked up within Jerusalem, his royal city, like a bird in a cage. I surrounded him with armed posts, and made it unthinkable (literally, "taboo") for him to exit by the city gate.

In the first prophetic story (B1), psychological pressure is added to the physical pressures brought on by the stringencies of the siege.

This account of the meeting of the two delegations (2 Kgs 18:17–36) was preserved in the prophetic circles of Isaiah's followers, and though it can hardly be considered a contemporary verbatim report of the events, especially the lengthy speech of the Assyrian Rabshakeh, it does contain many elements that derive from the original life setting. Taking part on the Assyrian side were the Tartan (lit. "second-in-command"; the commander-in-chief of the Assyrian army), the Rabsaris (lit. "chief eunuch"), and the Rabshakeh (lit. "chief cupbearer"); representing the Judeans were Eliakim son of Hilkiah, who was in charge of the palace, Shebnah, the scribe, and Joah son of Asaph, the recorder. The delegations met near the northern wall of Jerusalem, by the conduit of the upper pool, on the paved way to the Fuller's Field, and

Assyrian officer reading the terms of surrender from a scroll, from the opening of his armored vehicle at Pazashi; drawing of relief from Sargon's palace at Dur-Sharrukin (Khorsabad).

were within earshot of the Judean defenders on the city's wall. The Rabshakeh served as the spokesman for the Assyrian side and he is portrayed as having been fluent in Hebrew; his knowledge of Hebrew has suggested to some that he was a former Israelite, now in the service of Sennacherib. When asked by the Judeans to conduct the talks in Aramaic, the diplomatic language common in the West, the Rabshakeh turned down their request, explaining that his goal was to dissuade the Judean soldiers from continuing a struggle that was a foregone loss, and so he continued in Hebrew (2 Kgs 18:26–27).

Rabshakeh's rhetoric and argumentation were of high quality and many of those who heard him may have been moved by his reasoning. For example, he put forward: You cannot count on Egypt to aid your cause; it is nothing but a "broken reed of a staff, which will pierce the hand of anyone who leans on it." Perhaps by now word had reached Jerusalem that the Egyptian task force had been pushed back at Eltekeh, effectively ending its involvement in the fighting. Furthermore, the Assyrian argued, the Lord, God of Israel, would not protect Judah; after all, Hezekiah had removed His high places and altars (conceived to be a sacrilegious act). In fact, claimed Rabshakeh, it was the Lord who sent Sennacherib to destroy Judah. Therefore, the most prudent decision would be to surrender and stay alive. Don't be afraid of being taken off to exile, for you will live there in conditions very similar to those in Judah. "Live and do not die!" (2 Kgs 18:19–32).

The Judean ministers did not argue or negotiate with the Rabshakeh, but returned immediately to Hezekiah to report the terms demanded by Sennacherib. The king was overcome by fear because of what he heard, and in his anguish turned to Isaiah and asked for the prophet's intervention with the Lord. Isaiah ensured Hezekiah that Sennacherib "shall hear a rumor and return to his own land; I will cause him to fall by the sword in his own land" (2 Kgs 19:7). There is a break in the report at this point and the next we hear, is that the Assyrian monarch did withdraw from Jerusalem and returned to Nineveh, where once, "as he was worshiping in the house of his god Nisroch, his sons Adrammelech and Sharezer killed him with the sword, and they escaped into the land of Ararat. His son Esarhaddon succeeded him" (2 Kgs 19:37). Reference to the assassination of Sennacherib, which took place in 681, helps set the formulation of the events in this prophetic account to a generation or two after 701. Yet despite this late date, the account accurately recalls the impressive appearance of the Rabshakeh before the walls of Jerusalem and the retreat of Sennacherib.

The second prophetic account (B2) also concentrates on the events at Jerusalem and the Assyrian demand for surrender (2 Kgs 19:9b–35) and its author seems to have known the first account. Two of the personages of the first account, Hezekiah

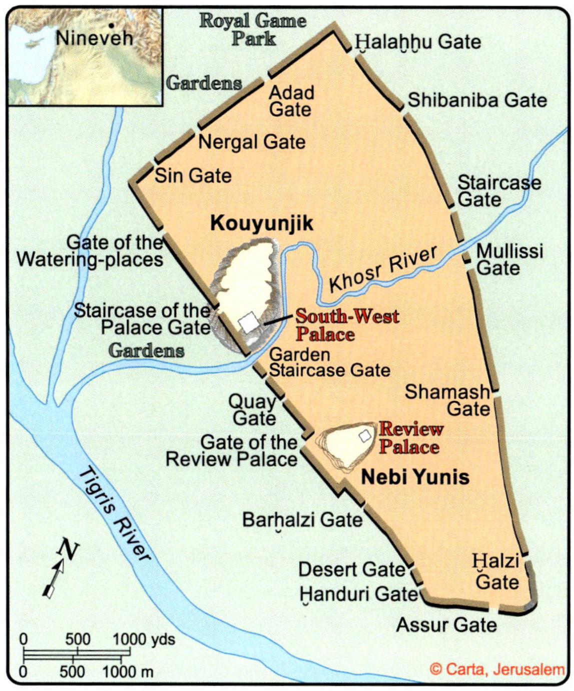

PLAN OF NINEVEH

(after Reade 1998–2001: 390)

and Isaiah, are active in the second telling, but they have different roles in this portrayal of the drama. This account begins with Sennacherib's call for surrender being brought in a letter delivered directly to Hezekiah by anonymous messengers. Upon reading the Assyrian demand, Hezekiah went straight away to the Temple with the letter in hand; he set it before the Lord and prayed for deliverance. Hezekiah argued: The blasphemous Assyrian king has called the Lord's position as the one and only God into question; divine action was needed immediately to redeem His fame. The prophet Isaiah came forward with the Lord's reply, set out in a lengthy diatribe against the empty boastings of the Assyrian king. In the end, Isaiah promised that Sennacherib "shall not come into this city, shoot an arrow there, come before it with a shield, or cast up a siege ramp against it. By the way that he came, by the same he shall return; he shall not come into this city, says the LORD. For I will defend this city to save it, for my own sake and for the sake of my servant David" (2 Kgs 19:32–34). And, indeed, that very night, the angel of the Lord cut down 185,000 Assyrian soldiers, whereupon Sennacherib broke camp and left for home.

As against these biblical traditions, Sennacherib's annals claim that the onerous siege of Jerusalem—where Hezekiah was locked up "like a bird in a cage"—brought Judah's king to his knees, and was followed by the delivery of an extremely heavy tribute to Nineveh after the departure of the Assyrian troops from Judah.

The End of the War and Its Aftermath

Despite the great discrepancies between the ancient sources, it may still be possible to suggest how the war in Judah ended. To critical modern thinking, the negotiations for Judah's surrender had apparently reached a settlement with which both sides could live. Such a settlement would have included the following points of agreement, drawn from both the Assyrian and biblical accounts: (1) Hezekiah would submit to Sennacherib, admitting to having broken his oath of loyalty to Assyria, and would recommit Judah to vassal status (cf. 2 Kgs 18:14; Rassam cylinder); (2) The siege of Jerusalem would be lifted and there would be no further assaults on the city; (3) Hezekiah would deliver a heavy indemnity, beyond the booty taken from the captured Judean cities (2 Kgs 18:15–16; Rassam cylinder); (4) Hezekiah would remain king of Judah; in reality his kingdom had been reduced in size; its rich agricultural region in the Shephelah was transferred to a number of Philistine cities (Rassam cylinder).

Such was the final accord that concluded the war in 701, and while it might have satisfied the parties to the conflict, it has caused much dissatisfaction among some modern historians, who hold that it should have ended otherwise, that is, the ancient sources are not to be believed. To their thinking, it is expected that Sennacherib would have extracted hasher terms from Hezekiah; after all, the Assyrian king held all the cards. Why did he compromise and leave the rebel Hezekiah on the throne, ruling in a capital that had not been conquered? This was against all the rules of war that Assyria followed! Therefore these modern skeptics suggest that either (1) the Assyrian and biblical sources refer to two different campaigns, one that ended with an Assyrian victory in 701 and one with a humiliating Assyrian retreat from Judah some years later, or (2) the Assyrian report of victory in 701 covers up an incomplete mission to Judah.

As to the first suggestion that there were two Assyrian campaigns against Judah, this proposal is without any documentary base whatsoever. No source tells of Sennacherib's return to the West after 701 at any time during the remaining twenty years of his reign. Had there been a second Assyrian campaign, and had it ended with a defeat of the Assyrian army, the history of the entire region would have to be reconfigured from the one presently accepted. A defeat would have meant that Sennacherib had lost the West, and Esarhaddon, his son and heir, would have had to undertake a campaign to the area in order to reassert Assyria's control. However upon taking the throne, Esarhaddon ruled over this area without having to engage in any military actions. Nor did Sennacherib's assassination and the upheavals in Assyria surrounding Esarhaddon's accession instigate uprisings. Assyria's western vassals remained submissive as a result of the destructive war in 701 BCE for at least the next quarter century.

As to the second suggestion that the Assyrian report (Rassam cylinder) of Hezekiah's submission cloaks with rhetoric what was in reality an Assyrian set-back in 701. This proposal assumes that had Sennacherib won, he would have removed the rebellious Hezekiah, replacing him with a more tractable vassal as was the usual Assyrian practice. Since this was not the case, this means that, in fact, for some unspecified reason, Sennacherib was unable to complete the takeover of Judah, specifically the capital Jerusalem. However, this deconstruction of the Assyrian text is based on a misreading of Assyria's goals in the West and undervalues the achievements of the war. Sennacherib had regained control of the major trade routes that ran from the border of Egypt through the Land of Israel northward, all of which passed through Assyrian provinces or vassal kingdoms. Having achieved that, he could be generous. He received renewed pledges of loyalty from the Philistine cities, and rewarded them with parts of the Judean Shephelah, rather than annexing the area as a new province. In similar fashion, once he received the submission of Hezekiah, who had been stripped of his most important holdings, he could leave him remain as vassal monarch over the backwater city of Jerusalem. There was no reason to expend military effort to capture a city whose economic importance to the empire was indeed minimal.

In sum, there was no second campaign and no cover-up. Judah and Hezekiah were roundly defeated once and for all in 701 BCE.

Carved figure of Sennacherib on the rock face of Judi Dagh in eastern Anatolia near the Tigris River (photo Timo Roller, via Wikimedia Commons).

EXCURSUS 1

HERODOTUS'S MICE AND SENNACHERIB

The tradition that the rescue of Jerusalem was the result of the killing of 185,000 Assyrian soldiers by the Angel of the Lord (2 Kgs 19:35) has been the subject of wonder for millennia. Pre-modern and modern readers alike have not been satisfied to leave this story as is, a classic example of a biblical miracle, but have sought to rationalize the Lord's dealings with the wicked. Flavius Josephus, the noted Jewish historian of the Second Temple period, expounded further for his Greek audience:

> When Sennacherib returned to Jerusalem from his war with Egypt, he found his force under Rabshakeh in danger from a plague, for God had visited a pestilential sickness upon his army, and on the first night of the siege one hundred and eighty-five thousand men had perished with their commanders and officers. By this calamity he was thrown into a state of alarm and terrible anxiety, and, fearing for his entire army, he fled with the rest of his force to his own realm, called the kingdom of Ninos (Nineveh). (*Antiquities* x 21–22)

The idea that a plague decimated the Assyrian army is still heard today. Only now, the explanation is dressed in environmental terms. Thus, for example, some suggest that the deaths were caused by the outbreak of disease due to the mean living conditions in the camp—the lack of basic sanitation—a frequent occurrence while on campaign.[18] More often reference is made to the report in Herodotus concerning Sennacherib's aborted invasion of Egypt.

> So presently came king Sennacherib against Egypt, with a great host of Arabians and Assyrians; and the warrior Egyptians would not march against him. The priest (Hephaestus, whose name was Sethos), in this quandary, went into the temple shrine and there bewailed to the god's image the peril which threatened him. In his lamentation he fell asleep, and dreamt that he saw the god standing over him and bidding him take courage, for he should suffer no ill by encountering the host of Arabia: "Myself," said the god, "will send you champions." So he trusted the vision, and encamped at Pelusium with such Egyptians as would follow him, for here is the road into Egypt; and none of the warriors would go with him, but only hucksters and artificers and traders. Their enemies too came thither, and one night a multitude of field mice swarmed over the Assyrian camp and devoured their quivers and their bows and the handles of their shields likewise, insomuch that they fled the next day unarmed and many fell. And at this day a stone statue of the Egyptian king stands in Hephaestus' temple with a mouse in his hand, and an inscription to this effect: "Look on me and fear the gods." (Herodotus, *Histories*, ii, 141)

Unfortunately, like many stories in this history, which were based on oral tales that Herodotus picked up as he travelled about the ancient world, this one conflates and distorts the facts of the case. The first Assyrian king to invade Egypt was not Sennacherib, but Esarhaddon, his grandson, who was aided in crossing the Sinai Peninsula by local Arab tribes (see *The Raging Torrent*, pp. 167–169). More significantly, the reason for the withdrawal of the Assyrian army was the lack of arms to engage the Egyptian forces, not a plague. In Greek folklore, mice are symbolic of the plague and the god Apollo Smintheus ("mouse") was at times depicted holding a mouse in his hand. It looks like Herodotus recast an Egyptian story he had heard in terms that were familiar to his Greek readers. And finally, not to be overlooked is the site of the disaster at Pelusium, a city on one of the easternmost arms of the Nile River, a considerable distance from the walls of Jerusalem in the Judean mountains.

In the end, it seems best not to associate the Herodotus report with the biblical tale. The victory of the Lord's angel over the Assyrian army should be understood on its own terms, the one understood by its first audience—a miraculous event carried out by Israel's God to save His devoted subjects.[19]

EXCURSUS 2

IN THE TRACKS OF THE JUDEAN DEPORTEES

While their brethren at home struggled through the difficult years of recovery that followed the calamitous events of 701 BCE, the Judeans who were deported by Sennacherib to Assyria—whatever their number—continued to fight a battle for existence, this one in a foreign land. Little is known about these first exiles from the kingdom of Judah. The Hebrew Bible neglects them altogether, while the Assyrian sources provide mere hints as to their fate.

A case in point are those Judean soldiers who were enlisted into the Assyrian army. Just as Israelite charioteers were mobilized by Sargon II as a select unit in his royal corps (see *The Raging Torrent*, no. 5.02), so, too, were fighters from Judah engaged as members of Sennacherib's heterogenous palace guard. One such Judean is depicted on a relief in the Southwest Palace at Nineveh, carrying a spear and shield; his identity as a Judean is confirmed by his distinctive dress, a Judean turban and a short skirt (see *Bound for Exile*, no. 5.012).

Judean laborers (in the second row), among other captives, hauling stone colossus from a quarry, as Assyrian supervisors look on; from Sennacherib's Southwest Palace at Nineveh (Courtesy of the Trustees of the British Museum).

More typical was the use made of the Judeans as laborers on state projects. Sennacherib prided himself in being the rebuilder of Nineveh that he converted in the capital of Assyria. All of his inscriptions refer to this immense undertaking, and explain the efforts expended in its accomplishment:

> The people of Babylon, the Arameans, and (people of) Mannea, Que and Cilicia, Philistia and the land of Tyre, who had not submitted to my yoke, I exiled them and had them carry the basket and make bricks. I cut down the canebrakes and reed marshes in Babylon and had their luxuriant reeds hauled by the enemy soldiers whom I captured for its (the palace) construction.
>
> (*The Raging Torrent*, no. 6.04)

(left) A Judean spearman (on right) in Sennacherib's royal guard, from Sennacherib's Southwest Palace at Nineveh (Courtesy of the Trustees of the British Museum).

10. THE SINGULARITY OF JERUSALEM

One hundred years after the war of 701 BCE that left Judah a devastated country, King Jehoiakim (605–598 BCE) and the leadership of the kingdom of Judah faced a political crisis similar to the ones his predecessors had faced many times in the past century; only now the object of contention was Babylonia, which had replaced Assyria as the hegemonic power in the West. The issue at hand was: rebel or remain loyal to Nebuchadnezzar? The risks were clear: defeat could lead to destruction and exile. The volatile atmosphere in Jerusalem in those days is described in the Book of Jeremiah, especially the heated debates at the gates of the Temple in which the prophet was the main protagonist (cf. Jer 7).

Jeremiah of Anathoth, prophet to king and people, called for a return to the Lord as the only way to save the kingdom, its capital and the Temple. Moreover, rebellion against Babylon was contrary to the Lord's plan and so would not succeed. The severity of this warning did not dissuade Jeremiah's audience, among whom were those who countered: Jerusalem, the chosen city of the Lord, was unassailable. History shows this for a fact. Had it not withstood the mighty Assyrian attack in the days of Hezekiah? And it would do so again. The prophet Micah—like Jeremiah—had spoken of great destruction, but in the end, Sennacherib retreated from the city and returned home where he was assassinated by his own sons. So while Jeremiah brought evidence for his case by referring to the destruction of the Lord's shrine at Shiloh centuries earlier (Jer 7:12), the Jerusalemites of the end of the seventh century held that their city enjoyed a special status, protected by the presence in its midst of the Lord's House: "This is the temple of the Lord, the temple of the Lord, the temple of the Lord" (Jer 7:4).

How did such opposing readings of history develop? Can the source of the belief in noble Jerusalem be traced? A review of the history of the seventh century is profitable in this regard.

As shown above, Judah at the turn of the eighth century was a defeated kingdom, brought to its knees by the Assyrian onslaught, deprived of much of its territory, with a considerable part of its population exiled; those that remained in the destroyed land were shackled with the payment of an enormous indemnity. Hezekiah did retain his throne, and though he ruled from the capital Jerusalem that had escaped the direct wrath of Sennacherib, he ruled a humbled and humiliated kingdom.

Isaiah's promise of recovery was a generation or two from fulfillment:

> And this shall be the sign for you: This year you shall eat what grows of itself, and in the second year what springs from that; then in the third year sow, reap, plant vineyards, and eat their fruit. The surviving remnant of the house of Judah

THE CAMPAIGNS OF NEBUCHADNEZZAR II, 605–601 BCE

Reconstruction of the Ishtar Gate of Babylon (photo Radomir Vrbovsky, via Wikimedia Commons).

shall again take root downward, and bear fruit upward; for from Jerusalem a remnant shall go out, and from Mount Zion a band of survivors. The zeal of the LORD of hosts will do this. (2 Kgs 19:29–31)

Archaeological surveys have uncovered signs from the mid-seventh century of the physical growth in Judah's highlands and semi-desert areas; in the hills and valleys surrounding Jerusalem, new farms and homesteads had been established, perhaps by Judeans who were displaced from the areas that had come under Philistine control.

While Judah struggled to its feet, events were taking place during the last decade of Sennacherib's reign in distant Babylon that effected the politics and social thought in Judah, especially as regards Jerusalem. Assyria under Sennacherib enjoyed only short periods of respite from the ongoing battles on its southern border against the Chaldeans and their Elamite allies. Ousting Merodach-baladan from Babylon was not enough to calm the spirit of rebellion. The six-year reign of Ashur-nadin-shumi, Sennacherib's son (699–694), as king in Babylon, ended with his being handed over to Elam where he apparently died. This act, more than any other, determined Babylon's fate. Sennacherib's vengeance against Babylon was great and when the city finally fell to Assyrian forces in 689 after years of battle, it suffered the most brutal treatment ever meted out to a captured city. If we are to believe the Assyrian description, Sennacherib literally wiped Babylon off the map.

In my second campaign, I marched quickly against Babylon which I was set upon conquering. Like the onset of a storm, I swept, (and) like a fog I enveloped it. I laid siege to that city; with mines and siege machines, I personally took it – the spoil of his mighty men, small and great. I left no one. I filled the city squares with their corpses. Shuzubu, king of Babylon, together with his family and his [ ], I brought alive to my land. I handed out the wealth of that city – silver, gold, precious stones, property and goods – to my people and they made it their own. My men took the (images of the) gods who dwell there and smashed them. They took their property and their wealth. Adad and Shala, the gods of Ekalate, which Marduk-nadin-aḫḫe, king of Babylon had taken and carried off to Babylon during the reign of Tiglath-pileser (I), king of Assyria, I brought out of Babylon and returned them to their place in Ekalate.

I destroyed and tore down and burned with fire the city (and) its houses, from its foundations to its parapets. I tore out the inner and outer walls, temples, the ziggurat of brick and earth, as many as there were, and threw them into the Araḫtu river. I dug canals through the city and flooded its place with water, destroying the structure of its foundation. I made its devastation greater than that of "the Flood." So that in future days, the site of that city, its temples and its gods, would not be identifiable, I completely destroyed it with water and annihilated it like inundated territory.

(*Context of Scripture*, vol. 2, p. 305)

The image of Marduk, Babylon's chief deity, was spared destruction and was carried off as spoil to Nineveh by the victorious Assyrians. In defense of Marduk's fame, the Babylonians explained this blatant desecration as the self-imposed exile of Marduk, who, angered by the wicked behavior of the Babylonians, abandoned his city to the wanton rampage of the Assyrians.

Now Babylon was not just another capital. It was the preeminent center of Babylonian culture, reaching back over a millennium to the days of King Hammurabi. Within its walls stood the Temple of Marduk, the Esagil, "House whose top is high," and its ziggurat (temple tower), the Etemmenanki, "House, the foundation of heaven and earth." The sacrilege exhibited in the annihilation of the city is unprecedented in the annals of Assyrian warfare. Of all the victories Sennacherib claimed, his actions in Babylon stand alone and would surely have convinced anyone who might have considered rebellion against Assyria that Sennacherib would brook no subordination.

Image of the god Marduk astride the snake-dragon on a cylinder seal of lapus lazuli. Its inscription states that it was dedicated by Marduk–zakir-shumi I (854–819 BCE), to be set in gold and hung around neck of the statue of Marduk in the Esagil temple.

The news of Babylon's destruction must have sent a shock wave throughout the Near East and it guaranteed Sennacherib a decade of untroubled rule. The reaction in Judah that was still licking its wounds from the defeat a decade earlier (see above, p. 32) could only have been amazement and consternation. Yet for some of Jerusalem's devotees another lesson was learned from the Babylonian tragedy. For them the idea that one of the world's great cities and Babylon's religious center could be destroyed and its god carried off to exile pointed up Jerusalem's specialness. This had been shown by the outcome of Judah's encounter with Assyria in 701. Jerusalem and only Jerusalem had stood up to Sennacherib and won. The city's salvation and the continued rule of a king of the Davidic dynasty were nothing less than miraculous, living proof of superiority of Israel's God. And as the seventh century wore on, other capital cities fell to Assyria, for example, Thebes in Egypt and Susa in Elam, convincing the Lord's faithful, the residents of Jerusalem, of their city's singular, protected position in the divine universe.

This sentiment dovetailed with the teaching of Isaiah, who had foreseen a time when the Temple of the Lord in Jerusalem would be predominate, attracting the nations to seek the Lord.

In days to come
the mountain of the LORD's house
shall be established as the highest of the mountains,
and shall be raised above the hills;
all the nations shall stream to it.
Many peoples shall come and say,
"Come, let us go up to the mountain of the LORD,
to the house of the God of Jacob;
that he may teach us his ways
and that we may walk in his paths."
For out of Zion shall go forth instruction,
and the word of the LORD from Jerusalem.
He shall judge between the nations,
and shall arbitrate for many peoples;
they shall beat their swords into plowshares,
and their spears into pruning hooks;
nation shall not lift up sword against nation,
neither shall they learn war any more. (Isa 2:2–4)

Aerial view of the Old City of Jerusalem today, looking north (photo Samuel Magal).

11. EPILOGUE

The three decades during which Hezekiah reigned were unlike any other in Judah's past, and consequently the past was of little help in assessing the challenges of the aggressive expansion of the Assyrian empire. Of the two Israelite kingdoms, Judah alone survived the imperial thrust that reached as far as the border of Egypt. Israel rebelled and was conquered and turned into an Assyrian province; Hezekiah, on the other hand, piloted the ship of state with competence for most of his years, all except for his decision to rebel against Sennacherib. The debacle that Judah suffered in 701—and surely that is what the military outcome of Sennacherib's campaign should be called—discredited Hezekiah in the eyes of many, despite his personal survival. At the cessation of hostilities, the stripped-down kingdom of Judah returned to Assyrian vassaldom and remained submissive for most of the seventh century. It was during the long reign of Hezekiah's son, Manasseh, who followed his father on the throne, that Judah entered the cosmopolitan cultural world that the empire fostered.

Yet all was not politics and war during the last quarter of the eighth century. Fresh breezes were blowing in Judah that challenged existing conceptions of ritual and morality. For example, the Deuteronomic teachings reinterpreted earlier law as now requiring a unified cult in the Lord's chosen city. This cult was to be imageless in complete repudiation of past tradition. And at the same time as the country's altars were being destroyed and pillars broken, prophets like Micah and Isaiah brought novel messages in the name of the Lord that criticized the Temple ritual, declaring it unwanted and useless. Just social behavior was the true "knowledge of the Lord."

It would take several generations for these new ideas to take root, and in the meantime, Hezekiah's iconoclastic and centralistic reforms were cancelled with the backing of Manasseh (2 Kgs 21:3–7). This rejection was likely twofold: it was an expression of disappointment with Hezekiah's foreign policy and disapproval of his cultic reforms. For many, Hezekiah had led Judah to estrangement from its God that consequently brought calamity upon all.

It was only due to retrospection—the distance that allows the later observer to re-evaluate past events and to see them in a new light—that the reputation of Hezekiah was rescued. Within a century, following the fluctuations in power and the final demise of Assyria, Hezekiah was remembered as pious and steadfast in his loyalty to the Lord, a model king for all ages.[20]

NOTES AND REFERENCES

1 Edward Hallett Carr, *What is History?*, New York 1961, p. 24.

2 S. Aḥituv, *Echoes from the Past*, Jerusalem 2008, pp. 318, 320, 322.

3 S. Aḥituv, *Echoes from the Past*, Jerusalem 2008, pp. 220–224.

4 The bibliography on the subject is large; for a sample of the discussion, see: J. H. Tigay, "A Second Temple Parallel to the Blessings from Kuntillet 'Ajrud," *Israel Exploration Journal* 40 (1990), p. 218; W. Dever, *Did God Have a Wife? Archaeology and Folk Religion in Ancient Israel*, Grand Rapids 2005; S. Aḥituv, E. Eshel, Z. Meshel, "The Inscriptions," in Z. Meshel, *Kuntillet 'Ajrud (Ḥorvat Teman): An Iron Age II Religious Site on the Judah–Sinai Border*, Jerusalem 2012, pp. 127–135.

5 No explanation for the restriction of sacrifice to a single site is given anywhere in the Deuteronomic legislation. J. H. Tigay surveys the suggested reasons offered by commentators. In the end, he considers that "the text masks a deeper reason that seemed inadvisable to reveal" (*Deuteronomy.The JPS Torah Commentary*, Philadelphia 1996, pp. 459–464).

6 Unless Hezekiah was out of step with the population of Judah, he would not have undertaken the cult reforms following his rebellion against Sennacherib, as national unity would have been a goal that the reforms undermined.

7 See Z. Herzog, "Tel Beersheba," in E. Stern (ed.), *The New Encyclopedia of Archaeological Excavations in the Holy Land*, Jerusalem 1993, vol. 1, pp.167–173.

8 See Z. Herzog, "Perspectives on Southern Israel's Cult Centralization: Arad and Beer-sheba," in R. G. Kratz and H. Spieckermann (eds.), *One God—One Nation. One God—One Cult: Biblical and Archaeological Perspectives*, New York 2010, pp. 171–199.

9 S. Aḥituv, *Echoes from the Past*, Jerusalem 2008, pp. 44–47. The restoration of the name is based on Isaiah's criticism of Shebnah in Isa 22:16.

10 E. Mazar, who discovered the king's seal, discusses the royal motifs in: Eilat Mazar, *The Ophel Excavations to the South of the Temple Mount 2009–2013, Final Reports Volume I*, Jerusalem 2015, pp. 635–638.

11 There is no way to identify clinically the disease from which Hezekiah suffered as the only symptom reported is that he had "boils." This Hebrew term covers a large variety of skin diseases ranging from eczema to pemphigus (which can be fatal).

12 This is the Assyrian name of the province that reflects the Aramaic pronunciation Shamarayin, also known from Ezra 4:10.

13 This is known from a later political-theological text (from the days of Esarhaddon?) that explores the "sin of Sargon" for which the king "was killed…and who was not interred in his house." See the recent discussion by S. C. Melville, *The Campaigns of Sargon II, King of Assyria, 721–705 B.C.*, Norman, OK 2016, pp. 187–191.

14 D. Gil, "The Geology of the City of David and its Ancient Subterranean Waterworks," in D. T. Ariel and A. De Groot (eds.), *Excavations at the City of David 1978–1985, Directed by Yigal Shilo, IV, Various Reports*, Qedem 35, Jerusalem 1996, pp. 1–28.

15 Despite the fact that the copy of the text in Isaiah displays a number of textual variations from the original, it does not substantially alter the picture presented.

16 T. R. Hobbs (*2 Kings*, Word Biblical Commentary 13, Waco, TX 1985, pp. 241–284) offers a harmonistic reading of 2 Kgs 18–19 as "a continuous story."

17 The date of the Rassam Cylinder establishes 701 BCE as the date of the campaign, it being the first Assyrian report of the western operations. The date "in the fourteenth year of King Hezekiah" given in 2 Kgs 18:13 for Sennacherib's advance against Judah is not easily coordinated with the Assyrian date of 701 if Hezekiah is found to have taken the throne in 727. It seems best to associate the "fourteenth year" with the tradition of the king's illness at the end of which he was gifted with an additional fifteen years (see p. 26). A different solution to this problem—lowering Hezekiah's sole reign by positing a co-regency with his father Ahaz—is broached by N. Na'aman, "Historical and Chronological Notes on the Kingdoms of Israel and Judah in the Eighth Century B.C.," *Vetus Testamentum* 36 (1986), pp. 83–91.

18 So, for example, W. von Soden, "Sanherib vor Jerusalem 701 v. Chr.," in G. A. Lehmann and R. Stiehl (eds.), *Antike und Universalgeschichte, Festschrift H. E. Stier*, Münster 1972, pp. 43–51; D. J. Wiseman, *1 & 2 Kings*, Tyndale Old Testament Commentaries, Leicester 1993, p. 284.

19 It is well to remember that the defeats of the Assyrian army go unrecorded in Assyrian documents. In some instances, such setbacks can be detected by the use of rhetorical analysis of the texts; in a few others, the non-Assyrian sources suggest defeat.

20 It must be admitted that not everyone subscribed to this praiseworthy evaluation. A short post eventum prophecy in the name of Isaiah laid the exile of Jehoiachin at the feet of Hezekiah (2 Kgs 20:16–19). Clearly this was not the view of the early Deuteronomistic author of Kings. The post-Exilic Chronicler adopted the Deuteronomistic approach and heaped further accolades upon Hezekiah by extending his reform activities, so that in the end, they came to resemble those of David and Solomon (cf. 2 Chron 29–30).

FOR FURTHER READING

Aḥituv, Shmuel. *Echoes from the Past: Hebrew and Cognate Inscriptions from the Biblical Period*, Jerusalem 2008.

Avigad, Nahman. *Discovering Jerusalem*, Jerusalem 1983.

Brinkman, John A. *Prelude to Empire. Babylonian Society and Politics, 747–626 B.C.*, Philadelphia 1984.

Cogan, Mordechai. "Sennacherib's Siege of Jerusalem. Once or Twice?" *Biblical Archaeology Review* 27 (2001), pp. 40–45, 69.

Cogan, Mordechai. "Sennacherib and the Angry Gods of Babylon and Israel," *Israel Exploration Journal* 59 (2009), pp. 164–174.

Cogan, Mordechai. *Bound for Exile: Israelites and Judeans under Imperial Yoke. Documents from Assyria and Babylonia*, Jerusalem 2013.

Cogan, Mordechai. *The Raging Torrent: Historical Inscriptions from Assyria and Babylonia relating to Ancient Israel*, 2nd ed., Jerusalem 2015.

Dubovsky, Peter. *Hezekiah and the Assyrian Spies: Reconstruction of the Neo-Assyrian Intelligence Services and its Significance for 2 Kings 18–19*, Rome 2006.

Eph'al, Israel. *The City Besieged: Siege and Its Manifestations in the Ancient Near East*, Jerusalem–Leiden 2009.

Gallagher, W. R. *Sennacherib's Campaign to Judah. New Studies*, Leiden 1999.

Geva, Hillel. "Western Jerusalem at the End of the First Temple Period in Light of the Excavations in the Jewish Quarter," in Vaughn and Killebrew 2003, pp. 183–208.

Geva, Hillel. "Jerusalem's Population in Antiquity: A Minimalist View," *Tel Aviv* 41 (2014), pp. 131–160.

Grabbe, Lester L. (ed.). *'Like a Bird in a Cage,' The Invasion of Sennacherib in 701 B.C.E.*, Sheffield 2003.

Hallo, William W. "Jerusalem under Hezekiah: An Assyriological Perspective," in Levine 1999, pp. 36–50.

Hallo, William W., and K. Lawson Younger. *Context of Scripture*, vol. 2, Leiden 2000.

Honor, Leo L. *Sennacherib's Invasion of Palestine. A Critical Source Study*, New York 1926.

Kalimi, Isaac, and Seth Richardson (eds.). *Sennacherib at the Gate of Jerusalem (701 B.C.E.): Story, History and Historiography*, Leiden 2014.

Levine, Lee I. *Jerusalem: Its Sanctity and Centrality to Judaism, Christianity, and Islam*, New York 1999.

Millard, Alan R. "Sennacherib's Attack on Hezekiah," *Tyndale Bulletin* 36 (1985), pp. 61–77.

NEAEHL. *New Encyclopedia of Archaeological Excavations in the Holy Land*. 4 vols. E. Stern (ed.), Jerusalem 1993.

Rainey, Anson F., and R. Steven Notley. *The Sacred Bridge: Carta's Atlas of the Biblical World*, Jerusalem 2006.

Reade, Julian E. "Ninive (Nineveh)," in *Reallexikon der Assyriologie*, vol. 9 (1998–2001), pp. 388–433.

Tadmor, Hayim. "Sennacherib's Campaign to Judah: Historiographical and Historical Considerations," in idem, *"With my many chariots I have gone up the heights of mountains": Historical and Literary Studies in Ancient Mesopotamia and Israel*, M. Cogan (ed.), Jerusalem 2011, pp. 653–675.

Ussishkin, David. *The Conquest of Lachish by Sennacherib*, Tel Aviv 1982.

Vaughn, Andrew G., and Ann E. Killebrew (eds.). *Jerusalem in Bible and Archaeology: The First Temple Period*, Leiden 2003.

Young, Robb A. *Hezekiah in History and Tradition*, Leiden 2012.